TECHNOLOGY INTEGRATION IN EDUCATION

TECHNOLOGY INTEGRATION IN EDUCATION

Editor
Prof. Ramesh Chandra

Publications

KALPAZ PUBLICATIONS
DELHI-110052

TECHNOLOGY INTEGRATION IN EDUCATION

Technology Integration in Education

Rs. 790

ISBN: 81-7835-234-6

This book is Vol. No. 6 of Universal Education and Technology in 21st Century (Set)

Published in 2005 in India by
Kalpaz Publications,
C-30, Satyawati Nagar, Delhi-110052
E-mail : Kalpaz@hotmail.com

Laser Typesetting at : Master Computers, Delhi
Printed at : Ajit Printers, Delhi

Contents

Preface

The introduction of technology into the classroom is changing the nature of delivering education to students from primary through to tertiary levels. Print literacy, although still widely used is gradually giving way to a new form of electronic literacy. More and more programs and education materials are becoming available in electronic form, more and more teachers are preparing materials in electronic form; and more and more students are generating papers, assignments and projects in electronic form. Blackboards are now being replaced by video projection screens, books with storage device servers and CDROMs as well as the emergence of online digital libraries. Even exams and grades are gradually becoming available through electronic means and notebooks are starting to give way to laptops. Also, students can be examined through computer managed learning systems and do tutorial exercises on a computer rather than in a classroom.

Such developments in education portray that there has been a shift from industrialisation to information based societies. Subsequently, technology is foreseeing a change in the education environment towards a reliance on electronic sources to deliver material. With such changes and the emergence of video conferencing and the internet, the barriers of distance are being broken down at a rapid rate, a key aspect of globalisation. Many institutions as direct providers of learning opportunities to students are using technology to deliver its programs, courses and tuition support. In fact, the information technology revolution is also foreseeing the development of new kinds of institutions such as 'virtual universities' which are delocalised across cyberspace, institutions with no real buildings and location as such, just web pages providing access to information, knowledge and ideas.

Countries are now realising the economic potential and value of technology in education. As such, it is vital that education systems embrace and implement technology into their schools to produce citizens capable of living in the twenty first century where technology is encroaching more and more into everyday life.

Editor

1

Assessment of Online Teaching

In the late 1990s, the new model of principals' training that has been used in York University's Principals' Qualification Program (PQP). One component of the program brings traditional case methodology into a computer-mediated/on-line environment. The on-line cases are narratives from the everyday lives of the Ontario school administrators who serve as mentors in the on-line environment.

The immediacy of classroom teaching and learning that forms the lived experience of teachers must be brought into the context of relationships and responsibilities that extend throughout the school, its communities and the bureaucratic relations linking the school to the educational system.

The principal must mediate these complex relationships. Indeed, complexity is one of the distinguishing features of the principalship. Traditionally, the work of the school principal has been to coordinate the relationships and tasks of the school with the community and the demands of the larger system in which the school is embedded.

In America, Ontario school teachers who are appointed as school principals must have completed (or be in the process of completing) the Principals' Qualification Program (PQP). It is a required preparatory program offered by most universities in Ontario and, recently, by the principals' associations. The York University PQP is accredited by the Ontario College of Teachers and is offered through the Field Development unit of the Faculty of Education.

York's PQP was completely revised in 1997, shifting the emphasis of the course toward relational leadership, leadership strategies for equity and diversity, and incorporating an action-research practicum. At any one time, 250–300 candidates are enrolled in the program. Ten to fifteen program facilitators teach in one of the two required programs at four course sites in the Greater Toronto Area. A focus on change at the school and system level is integrated into the program through the seminar topics and through an on-line mentoring process. A small, but important feature of the York PQP (14 out of 125 hours) is taught via computer-mediated communication to groups of candidates who converse on-line. In contrast to the course seminars, the on-line groups are not site-based.

PQP candidates are randomly assigned to online discussion groups. Each on-line group consists of 15 - 20 candidates who are mentored by two principals from different Boards of Education in the GTA. The On-Line Mentors are volunteers and represent a variety of Public and Catholic Boards. They are recruited for their knowledge and experience, and for their 'fit' with the underlying principles of the York PQP. Each week, the On-Line Mentors post cases for discussion drawn from their everyday experiences as principals. The on-line component of the program was developed for a number of reasons:

— To provide the opportunity for ongoing learning using computer-mediated technologies, including electronic mail and Internet information resources.

— To broaden the candidates knowledge of the range of issues and administrative practices of different Boards of Education across the GTA, for example to highlight differences between rural and urban schools, mono-cultural and multi-cultural schools, schools that are mono-lingual and those with a broad linguistic diversity.

— To extend the range of contacts so useful to recently appointed administrators.

— To provide a different learning medium for the candidates—one that is non-linear, reflective, and not tied to the schedules of face-to-face teaching and learning.

Computer-mediated discussion groups allow for interactions between experienced and aspiring administrators, mentoring relationships that no longer need to be confined to a single classroom or school. Indeed, the on-line technology allows for networking across the large distances of the GTA, and provides the opportunity for people working in diverse school situations to learn from each other through the discussion of cases drawn from the everyday experience of principals working across the diversity of GTA schools.

Case methodology has a long history in education for leadership and administration. It originated as an instructional technique at Harvard University Law School in 1870 and later became widely accepted in a variety of professional disciplines. A case as an account or description of a situation or sequence of events confronting an individual, a group of individuals, or an organization. Rather than deliver concepts and theories, cases (also called clinical correlation, leadership stories, real-life narratives, critical incidents, and vignettes) present situations for analysis about which decisions must be made. There are similarities of structure between case histories, clinical cases, problem-based learning and other experientially based methods in that they are all oriented to the particularities of practice while drawing on the generalities of theory.

The purpose of cases and case-based instruction in any professional field relates directly to the nature of the body of knowledge that exists in that particular field. For example, in teacher education cases are used to develop reflective practitioners and to promote teacher reflection and enhanced understanding. In the field of educational administration where decision-making skills are crucial, cases can offer opportunities to practice analysis, problem solving, action planning, and evaluation.

In the educational studies in general and in the area of school administration in particular the interest in the case methodology is manifested through a wide incorporation of and experimentation with case-based instruction in pre-service and in-service training of teachers and administrators.

At the university level, special centers have been established for research and promotion of the case methodology in the field of education (Pace University Center for Case Studies in Education is but one example). Likewise, educational journals devote a great deal of attention to this matter and provide a forum for discussion of the value of case methodology for preparation of educational cadre. For example, The Journal of Cases in Educational Leadership (JCEL) published by University of Utah is devoted solely to the publication of cases that can be effectively used in preparation of educational leaders.

Principal preparation programs have used case studies to remedy problems that arise in the gap between theory and practice. A major criticism of principal preparation programs has been: "Regardless of the year appointed, have been trained and certified as administrators through programs largely irrelevant to and grossly inadequate for the work responsibilities found in the school principalship".

The case methodology combines both artifactual and social elements. The artifactual component is the case itself, a description of an actual situation. The social component of case method is the discussion of the case by colleagues that usually takes the form of a case discussion (often referred to as a "case conference").

Case Methodology On-line

The emergence of computer-based technologies opened up new possibilities for case conferencing. The collision of technology and case methodology was inevitable. The combination of technology and case-based instruction gave birth to new applications of case methodology in teacher and principal preparation programs, for example video-cases, computer-based simulations, virtual case competitions on the World Wide Web, cases presented as CD-ROM and laser disks, and electronic meeting systems.

The technological formats of case analysis can be written, spoken, or based in hypermedia utilizing the Internet or World Wide Web. Unlike the traditional classroom discussion of cases, electronic meeting systems (EMS) allow for constant ongoing dialogue between participants. Moreover, electronic brainstorming produces significantly more fresh ideas than traditional classroom analysis of cases.

EMS also allows more people to interact without interruption and to input ideas simultaneously. Opportunity for the participation of all group members is also enhanced in computer-mediated case discussions. On-line case discussion in the York University PQP resonates with the need to decrease the gap between classroom instruction and practice and to enhance students' ability to make good decisions that are at the core of school leadership.

The PQP on-line cases are experiential narratives that focus on a broad set of concerns specific to the work of the principal. The cases, referred to by participants as scenarios, problems or situations, are posted weekly by the On-Line Mentors. Each week, candidates read the posted cases and respond to the issues, events and dilemmas of the case taking the perspective of a principal. This requires them to shift their reading of the cases from their experiential teaching horizon toward a one that encompasses the relationships within the school, the school community and the educational system with it's diverse participants. The role of case discussion facilitator is important in case methodology generally and the York PQP specifically. The facilitator guides the discussion by probing, directly challenging, or simply observing the discussion process.

Feedback plays an important role in the learning process: as people receive information about the results of their actions, they are able to correct themselves progressively until they achieve the intended results.

The PQP On-Line Mentors, all of whom were classroom teachers prior to becoming a principal, bring their knowledge of teaching and learning to the CMC environment. They provide feedback in the form of comments addressed to candidates' responses, suggestions for different presentation strategies, ideas for deepening the responses, or concluding thoughts.

The On-Line Mentors also direct discussions and monitor candidates' participation in order to facilitate discussions that are reflective and thoughtful. In order to make case discussions challenging, educative and interesting, On-Line Mentors may make suggestions and ask questions related to the posted case. The on-line narratives are written rather than oral interactions, often presented in a laconic and point specific form rather than lengthy and comprehensive manner. The audiences for whom the narratives are constructed are other educators attending or teaching the course.

Although one face-to-face meeting of the on-line groups is scheduled during the course, candidates may never meet their on-line mentor or other members of their on-line group. Group cohesion is developed through a combination of required participation, the skill of the on-line mentor, and the ongoing involvement of the participants. Case methodology has changed in recent years from the method of instruction based on face-to-face discussion of oral cases/narratives confined to the classroom space to computer-mediated asynchronous discussion of on-line cases in virtual classrooms/cyber-classrooms.

Narratives in cyberspace, rather than being a part of an oral discourse, entail new communicative styles and ways of engagement with texts/cases on the part of the learners. In theorizing of learning, claims have been made that we learn from the other's response to what we convey. Thus, learning the art of school leadership through on-line narratives necessitates the learners to put their responses out there and to find out what comes back.

A unique feature of the York PQP cases posted on-line is that often they present an account of events that happened in the same week (or sometimes even the same day) as the case is posted for discussion. While varying in content and length, the cases are authentic narratives from the work experience of GTA principals. As such, they have some pedagogical similarity to more traditional principal training methods such as "inbox" and "shadowing" exercises.

Some of the cases posted by On-Line Mentors open up with the words like: "Just a quick situation we had at our school this week that caused us some thought" or "Here is the situation based on a real case that happened recently." The fact that cases posted for discussion are "fresh" cases enables On-Line Mentors to enrich the dialogue by adding new details and nuances to the case and informing participants about the trajectory of events.

The use of narratives brings into view the implicit and explicit ethical and moral issues that permeate the stories of schooling. Narratives bring the complexity of the coordinated stories about school leadership and administration to the medium of on-line group learning. Equally important, they allow beginners "to consider and inspect the informal or tacit systems which exist side-by-side with the formal manifest systems operating in schools and organizations'. One of the program challenges that confront PQP candidates and their program teachers are to develop the skill to see the case narratives through the eyes of an administrator rather than a teacher.

In the on-line mentor responses, we see a complex teaching and learning about the social and professional mores of the principalship. As the course progresses, candidates felt freer to speak from their professional experiences in the teaching profession and from their life experiences as people interested in education. Bringing their life experiences to bear on an administrative framework, students came up with diverse (often even polar) responses and felt free to disagree with one another. The consensual uniformity of candidates' standpoints was less present in the analysis of the cases that dealt with ethical concerns or involved moral judgements.

The analysis of the PQP on-line narratives, student responses to less complex and more transparent cases often resulted in producing collective virtual texts where each ensuing individual script, more or less, echoed the line of thinking developed in responses posted earlier. In contrast, the responses to case narratives that drew on local experience with ethical issues embedded in the stories did not turn into unitary, virtual texts—one-best solution—produced by collective efforts of on-line participants.

Large-Scale Assessment and Internet

In the United States, Large-scale assessment is undergoing enormous pressure to change. That pressure stems from many causes. Depending upon the type of test, the issues precipitating change include an outmoded cognitive-scientific basis for test design; a mismatch with curriculum; the differential performance of population groups; a lack of information to help individuals improve; and inefficiency. These issues provide a strong motivation to reconceptualize both the substance and the business of large-scale assessment.

At the same time, advances in technology, measurement, and cognitive science are providing the means to make that reconceptualization a reality. In the same way that it is already helping to revolutionize commerce, education, and even social interaction, the Internet will help revolutionize the business and substance of large-scale assessment. Whether for educational admissions, school and student accountability, or public policy, large-scale assessment in the United States is undergoing enormous pressure to change. This pressure is most evident with respect to high-stakes tests, like those used for grade promotion or college entrance.

For achievement surveys like NAEP, which offer no information to individuals, schools, or districts, motivation to participate is undoubtedly diminished. Testing programs are expensive to operate. That expense gets passed on to taxpayers for a state or federal test like NAEP, or directly to examinees in the case of admissions measures. Further, to be maximally useful, test results are needed quickly. Rapid information delivery is certainly a requirement in the education policy arena, where the results of national surveys may sometimes take years to produce. It is also increasingly true in the admissions context, where more rapid feedback is needed not only for early decisions, financial aid, and the rolling acceptances that are beginning to characterize some distance learning programs, but also for guidance and placement.

Radical improvements in assessment will derive from advances in three areas technology, measurement, and cognitive science. Of the three, new technology will be the most influential in the short term. New technology will have the greatest influence because it—not measurement and not cognitive science—is pervading our society. Billions of dollars are being invested annually to create and make commonplace powerful, general technologies for commerce, communications, entertainment, and education. Due to their generality, these technologies can also be used to improve assessment. These technological advancements revolve primarily around the Internet. The Internet is (or will be) interactive, broadband, switched, networked, and standards-based.

Interactive means that we can present a task to a student and quickly respond to that student's actions. Switched means that we can engage in different interactions with different students simultaneously. In combination, these two characteristics (interactive and switched) make for individualized assessments. Broadband means that those interactions can contain lots of information. For assessment tasks, that information could include audio, video, and animation. Networked indicates that everything is linked. This linkage means that testing agencies, schools, parents, government officials, item writers, test reviewers, human scorers, and students are tied together electronically. That electronic connection can allow for enormous efficiencies.

The standards-based means that the network runs according to a set of conventional rules that all participants follow. That fact permits both the easy interchange of data and access from a wide variety of computing platforms, as long as the software running on those platforms (e.g., Internet browsers), adheres to those rules too.

Internet affords the potential to deliver efficiently on a mass scale individualized, highly engaging content to almost any desktop; get data back immediately; process it; and make information available anywhere in the world, anytime day or night. Paper delivery cannot compete with this potential. The Internet is, of course, not being built to service the needs of large-scale assessment. It is, instead, being built for e-commerce: to sell products and services over the web to consumers and to businesses directly.

Coincidentally, the capabilities needed for e-commerce are essentially those needed for e-assessment:

— interactive (so that products can be offered and orders transacted),

— switched (so different business transactions can be conducted with different customers simultaneously),

— broadband (so that those offers can be as engaging and enticing as possible),

— networked (so that product offers, orders, shipping, inventory, and accounting can be integrated), and

— standards-based (so that everyone can get to it, regardless of computing platform).

By any measure, the Internet and use of it, has grown dramatically, to say the least. As a communications medium, the Internet last year surpassed the telephone, with 3 billion email messages sent each day. The number of unique URLs (web-page directory and subdirectory addresses) has grown from just under a billion in 1998 to a projected 3 billion in 2000.

In the United States, the percentage of homes with Internet access has increased from 26% in December 1998 to 42% in August 2000. Worldwide, the number of users has grown from somewhere between 117 to 142 million in 1998 to about 400 million in 2000. Finally, the number of host computers has gone from about 30 million to 75 million from January 1998 to January 2000. This phenomenal growth may slow as investment subsides from the speculative rates of the past few years. However, the vast size of the Internet and its user base constitute a critical mass that should continue to attract substantial capital. For commerce, the promise of the Internet is all about being faster, cheaper, and better.

Two "laws" of the digital era illustrate this promise. Moore's Law predicts the doubling of computational capability (specifically, at the level of the microchip) every 18 months. As Negroponte has explained, what filled a room yesterday is on your desk today and will be on your wrist tomorrow. Metcalfe's Law says that the value of a network increases by the square of the number of people on it.

The true value of a network is, thus, less about information and more about community. One can see this effect clearly in eBay, the online auction broker. Each new user potentially benefits every other existing user because every eBay member can be both buyer and seller. Metcalfe's law is playing out well beyond eBay. Online business-to-business auction brokers are appearing in a variety of industries, including natural gas, electricity, steel, and bandwidth. Another illustration of this cheaper-faster-better result is the effect of the

Internet on the traditional relationship between richness and reach, where richness is the depth of the interaction that a business can have with a customer and reach is the number of customers that a business can contact through a given channel. Traditionally, one limited the other. That is, a business could attain maximal reach but only limited richness.

For example, through direct mail, broadcast, or newspaper ads a company could communicate with many people but have a meaningful interaction with none of them. Similarly, a business could attain maximal richness but limited reach. Via personal contact (e.g., door-to-door sales), very deep interactions can occur, but with only a relatively small number of people. What has the Internet done? It has transformed the relationship between richness and reach by allowing businesses to touch many people in a personalized but inexpensive way. It makes for mass customization.

There are two major dimensions to reinventing assessment. One is the business of assessment. This dimension centers on the core processes that define an enterprise. In many cases, those core processes can become many times more efficient because moving bits is faster and easier than moving atoms; that is, electronically processing information is far more cost effective than physically manipulating things.

For large-scale testing programs, some examples of the potential for electronic processing are in:

— developing tests, making the items easier to review, revise, and automatically morph into still more items because the items themselves are digitally represented;

— delivering tests, eliminating the costs of printing, warehousing, and shipping tons of paper;

— presenting dynamic stimuli like audio, video, and animation, making the need for specialized testing equipment (e.g., audio cassette recorders, VCRs) obsolete;

— transmitting some types of complex constructed responses to human graders, removing the need to transport, house, and feed the graders;

— scoring other complex constructed responses automatically, reducing the need for human reading et al.,; and

— distributing test results, cutting the costs of printing and mailing reports.

Encyclopaedia Britannica was established in Scotland in 1768. It is the oldest and most famous encyclopedia in the English-speaking world. By 1990, its sales had reached $650 million per annum. But then suddenly, Britannica's fortunes drastically changed.

In 1996, the company was sold for less than half its net worth (i.e., the value of its assets, including its encyclopedia inventory, minus its liabilities). That same year, it eliminated its entire door-to-door North American sales force. What happened was that the reference book business was reinvented because of the emergence of new technology. At its peak, Britannica was a 32-volume set of books costing well over $1,000.

In 1993, Microsoft introduced Encarta on CD-ROM for under $100 and even though Britannica was much more comprehensive, the difference for most people wasn't worth an extra $900+. Initially, Britannica did not respond as it didn't take the threat from Encarta seriously. But when it did respond, it did so ineffectively because Britannica wouldn't fit on a single CD-ROM and because the company's large sales force wasn't suited to selling software.

But, ultimately, Britannica wasn't ready to cannibalize its existing paper business to enter this new electronic one. Why is this story important? It's important because similar (though less extreme) scenarios are playing themselves out now in individual investing, book selling, travel planning, music distribution, long distance telephony, and even business-to-business transactions. (As to the last, Cisco Systems makes 90% of its revenue from business-to-business transactions done over the Internet.

These reinvention scenarios are forcing organizations—including some in educational assessment—to come quickly to grips with where new technology will and will not help core business processes. As should be obvious, technology-driven changes in business processes can occur quickly and their consequences can be significant for the organizations that service a particular market. In fact, if radical and pervasive enough, process changes can force shifts in the substance of the business itself.

So, although reinventing the business of assessment by incorporating technology into specific assessment processes is about trying to achieve the efficiencies needed to remain competitive today, reinventing the substance of assessment—most fundamentally, the reason we do it—is not about today. It's about tomorrow.

The populations seeking education are changing and so are their purposes for learning. At the college level, just 16% of students fit the traditional profile: 18-22 years old, full-time, on-campus resident. This is not because fewer 18-22 year olds are going to college. It is because more adults are. The adult cohort is, in fact, the fastest growing segment in postsecondary education.

Working adults over age 24 constitute some 44% of college students. Over the past 25 years, employer demand in the U.S. has shifted toward higher educational qualifications, as indicated by an increasing premium paid for those with a college degree. But in addition to this rise in entry qualifications, the knowledge required to maintain a job in many occupations is changing so fast that 50% of all employees' skills are estimated to become outdated within 3-5 years.

Witness any job that requires interaction with information technology (IT), which is a growing proportion of jobs. In fact, by 2006 almost half of all workers will be employed by industries that are either major producers or intensive users of IT products and services. So, more people want postsecondary education because they need to have it if they want to become—and stay—employed. And, more of these individuals are nontraditional students who may work, travel in their jobs, or have families. This population's unmet educational need is increasingly becoming the target of distance learning.

According to the National Center for Education Statistics, between fall 1995 and 1997-98, the percentage of higher education institutions offering distance learning courses increased by one-third, and the number of course offerings and enrollments approximately doubled. But although many institutions have delivered distance learning via mail, radio, or television for years, this growth is not in those media. Rather, it is distance learning via the Internet that is booming.

Among all higher-education institutions offering any distance learning, the percentage of institutions using asynchronous Internet-based technologies nearly tripled, from 22% in 1995 to 60% in 1997-1998. More recent data from Market Data Retrieval (MDR) confirm the trend. MDR relates that, as of the 1999-2000 academic year, 34% of two- and four-year colleges offered accredited degree programs via computer, up from 15% the year before. As of 2000, U.S. institutions reportedly offered more than 6,000 accredited courses on the Web and, by 2002. over 2 million students will be enrolled, a tripling of the 1998 enrollment. At the same time, Internet-based distance learning is finding its way into high school.

The need is generated by home-schooled students (of which there are over 1 million in the US), districts without a full complement of qualified teachers, and the children of migrant workers. So-called "virtual high schools" have emerged in Alabama, Arizona, California, Florida, Illinois, Indiana, Kentucky, Maryland, Massachusetts, Michigan, Missouri, Nebraska, New Mexico, and Utah. These programs can cross state lines, with offerings open to students regardless of residence. Of particular note is that both the University of Missouri at Columbia High School and the Indiana University

High School have been granted accreditation by the North Central Association of Colleges and Schools. Accreditation means that students can apply course grades earned through these online institutions toward their high-school graduation.

The growth of Internet-based distance learning will have a significant impact upon traditional education. For one, it may threaten the existence of established institutions. Many in the private sector see education as a huge industry that produces mediocre results for a high cost. If the private sector can leverage new technologies, like distance learning, to deliver greater value, the institutions that dominate education today will not be the leaders tomorrow.

The rapid growth of for-profit education companies, and the seemingly endless creation of well-capitalized new ones, suggests that a serious challenge to the existing order is well underway. The gravity of the threat is evident in how non-profits have responded. A second reason that the growth of Internet-based distance learning will influence traditional education is that regardless of its impact on nonprofit institutions, the distance learning industry will produce sophisticated software that everyone can use, in school and out.

The considerable potential of online learning—local or distance—is reflected in a report to the President and Congress of the bipartisan Web-Based Education Commission. The question is no longer if the Internet can be used to transform learning in new and powerful ways. The Commission has found that it can. Nor is the question should we invest the time, the energy, and the money necessary to fulfill its promise in defining and shaping new learning opportunity. As online learning becomes more widespread, the substance and format of assessment will need to keep pace.

So, as students do more and more of their learning using technology tools, asking them to express that learning in a medium different from the one they typically work in will become increasingly untenable, especially where working with the medium is part of the skill being tested. These changes in learning methodology offer exciting possibilities for assessment innovation. On site or off, an obvious result of delivering courses via the Internet is the potential for embedding assessment, perhaps almost seamlessly, in instruction.

Since students respond to instructional exercises electronically, their responses can be recorded, leaving a continuous learning trace. Depending upon how the course and the assessment are designed, this information could conceivably support a sophisticated model of student proficiencies. That model might be useful both for dynamically deciding what instruction to present next and for making more global judgments about what the student knows and can do at any given point. In addition to assessment embedded in Internet-delivered courses, one can imagine Internet-delivered-assessment embedded in traditional classroom activity.

Such assessment might take the form of periodically delivered exercises that both teach and test. In this scenario, the exercises would be standardized and performance might serve, depending upon the level of aggregation, to indicate individual, classroom, school, district, state, or national achievement. Thus, these exercises could serve summative as well as formative purposes and be useful to individuals as well as institutions.

A continuing concern with such reinvention visions is whether schools (and students) are ready technologically and, in particular, what to do about technology differences across social groups. The National Center for Education Statistics (NCES) reports that as of September 1999, 95% of schools were connected to the Internet, up from 35% in 1994.

Schools in all categories, (i.e., by grade level, poverty concentration, and metropolitan status), were equally likely to have Internet access. Further, most schools had dedicated lines: only 14% were using dial-up modem, a slower and less reliable access method. Clearly many of these schools could have only a single connected machine and that machine could be the one sitting on the principal's desk.

According to NCES, as of September 1999, 63% of all instructional rooms had Internet access (up from 3% in 1994, a 20-fold increase in five years). The ratio of students to Internet-connected computers was 9:1, down from 12:1 only a year earlier. These are staggering numbers, for they imply that classrooms are connecting to the Internet at a very rapid rate. This success is in no small part due to federal efforts.

The government's e-rate program has been giving public schools and libraries discounts of up to 90% on phone service, Internet hook-ups, and wiring for several years ("FCC: E-rate subsidy funded," 2000). In total, the program has committed 3.65 billion dollars to over 50,000 institutions, helping connect more than one million public school classrooms. In addition, 70% of the program's last round of funding went to schools in the lowest income areas. However, even with these very significant efforts, there continue to be equity issues. As of September 1999, in high poverty schools, the ratio of students to Internet computers was 16 to 1.

Certainly, with few exceptions, it would be impossible to deliver large-scale assessment via the Internet today. But the trend is clear: the infrastructure is quickly falling into place for Internet delivery of assessment to schools, perhaps first in survey programs like NAEP that require only a small participant sample from each school, but eventually for inclusive assessments delivered directly to the desktop.

As evidence, witness the requests-for-proposals recently released by the state education departments of Oregon, Virginia, and Georgia for building Internet-delivered, state-assessment systems. Assuming that every classroom is wired, will all students then have the technology skills needed to take tests on-line? Clearly, more students are becoming computer-familiar every day and developing such skills is a national educational technology goal.

But, as Negroponte suggests, computer familiarity is really the wrong issue. The secret to good interface design is to make it go away. Thus, advances in technology will eventually eliminate the need to be computer familiar. After nomadic computing, which we are now entering with the proliferation of wireless Internet devices and personal digital assistants, comes ubiquitous computing—the embedding of new technology into everyday items.

Inventions like "radio" paper may allow students to interact with computers in the same way that they interact with paper today. Smart desks are another likelihood, in which case a test may be electronically delivered, quite literally, to every desktop. In the U. S., then, we may see a future in which every classroom is wired and every student can easily take tests on line.

To be sure, the Internet is an American phenomenon. It derives from research sponsored by the Defense Department in the 1960's. As a result of this history, the overwhelming majority of users were, until very recently, from our shores. At this writing, over 60% of Net users reside outside of the United States and the foreign growth rate now exceeds the domestic one. The largest numbers of foreign Internet users are, of course, in developed nations. These nations have the telecommunications infrastructure and citizens with enough disposable income to afford the trappings of Internet use.

The challenges for these nations are undoubtedly great. Over time, however, we should see significant progress in building the infrastructure and the user base here too. This progress will occur for at least two reasons. First, the cost of technology has been dropping precipitously and, by Moore's law, will continue to decline. Further, because the future of computing is undoubtedly in wireless devices, a telecommunications infrastructure will be much cheaper to acquire than the land-lines of old.

Metcalfe's law suggests, markets will become all the more valuable as they are interconnected. (Witness the global economy and the economic benefits resulting to nations from integration with it.) That developing nations join the e-commerce network means greater opportunity for all. It means more vendor choice for the people of developing nations; more opportunity for developed nations to serve these markets; and a new opportunity for third-world businesses themselves to compete globally.

The Internet will make it easier for developing nations to get access to assessment services from elsewhere and for those nations to distribute their own assessment services regionally or around the world. This ease of access and distribution should make it possible to form international consortia. Such consortia will be able to assemble technical resources that a single nation might not be able to acquire.

In addition, those consortia may be able to purchase services from others more efficiently than nations could obtain individually. Finally, an electronic network should make it easier to participate in international studies, bringing the benefits of benchmarking to nations throughout the world.

One of the largest instantiations of technology-based assessment to date is computer-based testing (CBT) in postsecondary admissions. As programs like the Graduate Record Examinations, the Graduate Management Admission Test, and the Test of English as a Foreign Language have found, CBT can be enormously costly.

Being among the first large-scale programs to move to computer, they bore the brunt of creating the infrastructure for what was essentially a new business. The building of that infrastructure was initiated in the early 1990's before test developers knew how to create tests for computer, before computers were widely available for individuals to take tests on, and before the Internet was ready to bring those tests to students.

In essence, these programs needed to build both a factory to stamp out a new product and a new distribution mechanism. A first generation infrastructure now exists, but it is not yet optimized to produce and deliver tests as efficiently as possible. If we have learned anything from the history of innovation, it is that new technologies are often initially far too expensive for mass use. That was true of the automobile, telephone service, commercial aviation, and the personal computer, among many other innovations.

For example, in 1930 the cost of a three-minute telephone call from New York to London was $250. By 1995, the cost had dropped to under $1. As a second instance, when the IBM Personal Computer was introduced in 1981, it cost around $5,000. At the time, the median family income in the United States was on the order of $25,000, so that a computer cost about 20% of the average family's earnings—not very affordable. At this writing, the cost of a computer with many times greater capability is a little more than $500 and the median income is closer to $55,000.

A computer now costs about 1% of average income. When a promising new technology appears, individuals and institutions invest, allowing the technology to evolve and a supporting infrastructure to develop. Over the course of that development, failures inevitably occur. Eventually, the technology either dies or becomes commercially viable—that is, efficient enough. At this point, it's an impressive list including non-profit testing agencies, for profit-testing companies, school districts, state education departments, government agencies, and companies with no history in testing at all.

Sustaining technologies enhance the performance of established products in ways that mainstream customers have traditionally valued. Historically, most technological advances in any given industry have been sustaining ones (e.g., in the personal computer industry, faster chips and bigger, higher-resolution monitors).

Occasionally, disruptive technologies emerge. Companies introduce these technologies hoping their features will provide competitive edge. However, these features characteristically overshoot the market, giving customers more than they need or are willing to pay for. Thus, disruptive technologies result in worse product performance, at least in the near-term, on key dimensions in a company's established markets.

Interestingly, a few fringe customers typically find a disruptive technology's new features attractive. In these niche markets, such technology may thrive. If and when it advances to the level and nature of performance demanded in the mainstream market, the new technology can invade it, rapidly knocking out the traditional technology and its dependent practitioners.

CBT has many of the characteristics of a disruptive technology. Established testing organizations are applying it in their mainstream markets, most notably postsecondary admissions. This innovation was introduced, in good part, to provide competitive edge through features like the ability to take a test at one's convenience and to get score reports immediately. As it turned out, these features overshot the market.

At least initially, registrations for continuously-offered computer-based admissions tests mirrored those for fixed-date administrations, suggesting that scheduling convenience was not a highly valued feature in the market of the time.

Moreover, examinees were dissatisfied with losing some of the features of paper exams, including the ability to proceed through the test nonlinearly, the option to review the scoring of items actually taken, and the low cost. Although it encountered difficulty in the mainstream admissions testing market, CBT found more rapid acceptance in the niches.

One example is information technology (IT) certification, which individuals pursue to document their competence in some computer-related proficiency. In 1999, over three million examinations in 25 languages were administered in this market.

Most of these tests were delivered on computer and most were offered on a continuous basis. Let's start by asking what features a testing product must have to succeed in this niche. First, it must be continuously offered because these test candidates build technology skill on their own schedules—at home or on the job, very often through books or online learning. These individuals want to test when they are ready, not when the testing companies are. Second, such a test must generally be offered on computer since technology use is the essence of the certification.

Security is not as critical as in admissions testing, so large item pools are not needed, reducing production cost. Lower security is tolerable because if an individual appears on the job with a dishonestly obtained credential but without the required skill, he or she will not last. Finally, test volume is self-replicating: there are many repeat test takers because information technology changes rapidly, so skills must be updated constantly.

From an innovation perspective, then, IT certification may be one context in which the CBT of today can flourish and develop to better meet the needs of other assessment markets. Industry leaders often fail precisely because they attempt to introduce disruptive technologies into major markets before it's time. The Industry leaders do not pursue those opportunities to refine the technology. Instead, they give up, having run out of resources or credibility.

Making a disruptive technology work requires iteration and iteration means failure. Because they risk neither large resources nor reputations in the mainstream market, it is the fringe players who can fail early, often, and inexpensively enough to eventually challenge and overtake the industry leaders.

Future of Technology Based Assessment

The online learning will become a major enterprise, especially for the lifelong updating of skills. In this market, institutions will be less concerned with questions of who gets in and more with who gets out, and what it is they have to do to get out. Because once hired, businesses are becoming more concerned with what employees know and can do, and less with where they went to school. Similarly, individuals are becoming more concerned with finding course offerings that meet their skill development goals and less with whether those offerings come from one institution or a half-dozen. The assessment need at first, it is for knowledge facilitation and, second, for knowledge certification; that is, to help people develop their skills and then document that they've developed them.

The challenge is to figure out how to design and deliver embedded assessment that provides instructional support and that globally summarizes learning accomplishment. In other words, the challenge is to combine richness with reach to achieve mass customization—use the Internet's ability to deliver the richness of customized assessment to reach a mass audience.

Certainly, we can dynamically adapt along a global dimension, as is done in many of today's computerized tests. But as we move assessment closer to instruction, we should eventually be able to adapt to the interests of the learner and to the particular strengths and weaknesses evident at any particular juncture, as intelligent tutors now do.

Likewise, we should be able to customize feedback to describe the specific proficiencies the learner evidenced in an instructional sequence. But perhaps the most far-reaching customization of assessment will come through modular online courses, whereby an instructor—or even a sophisticated learner—assembles a series of components into a unique offering. The Department of Defense (DOD) has taken a significant step through the Sharable Courseware Object Reference Model (SCORM).

SCORM is to embody specifications and guidelines providing the foundation for how DOD will use technology to build and operate the learning environment of the future. SCORM will allow mixing and matching of learning segments to create lower cost, reusable training resources.

2

Effective Open Learning Process

The process of constructing open learning communities suggests moving away from forms of education which emphasize knowledge transmission towards a culture of learning. The concept of open learning communities believes in the creative potential of human beings to interact and collectively reshape and reconstruct the world.

The activities of community groups and non-governmental organizations involved in the fields of development and education there is some evidence that they have been among the first to question narrow and limiting educational frameworks and approaches.

They have taken action and set up alternative education programs outside the formal system. They have worked with those learners who have either dropped out of the formal system or never had access to it in the first place - the majority of whom are women. They have been the advocates and practitioners of emancipatory learning, emphasizing learning as a process of 'conscientization' leading to an understanding of where one's place in the world is in relation to existing power structures.

The ideological, practical and relational dynamics among the groups of NGOs involved in education and development may provide valuable insights to the question in how far these actors are involved in and contribute to the process of conceptualizing and putting into practice open learning communities.

The analytic value of the term non-governmental organizations is limited. EFA NGOs just like NGOs in general differ with regard to motivation, organizational structure and culture, hierarchical structure, areas and scope of action, status, size, historical and geopolitical context, membership and - most importantly, with regard to political/ philosophical/ ideological orientation.

Some are exclusively service-providers, others are voluntary organizations. Some are mainly intermediaries, others grassroots associations. Depending on the location of an NGO's headquarters, some are considered Northern NGOs (headquarters based in the North) and some Southern NGOs; some are international in scope, others regional, national or local.

This diversity can be found among NGOs involved in education and development just as for any other group of NGOs. Any labelling of a group runs the risk of undermining the diversity of its membership. Still, for strategic or other reasons, different groups may chose to regroup under a common label and draw attention to their shared ideas and goals. In the case of the NGOs involved in education and development, an important and unifying reference point in the recent history of education and development has been the Education for All initiative. This initiative goes back to the World Conference on Education for All, also referred to as the Jomtien Conference, in 1990 where NGOs for the first time were officially recognized by governments and international agencies as partners in the field of education and development.

The main outcome of the Conference was the adoption of an action plan which committed UN agencies, member states and NGOs to consider Education for All the priority area for the ten years to come in order to make the right to education a reality for all. The Jomtien Conference also had some unintended side effects which proved to be particularly important for the international NGO community.

The Conference provided a space and an occasion for NGOs involved in education and development to either strengthen their existing networks or to create new NGO structures. In light of the dynamics triggered among NGOs within the context of the World Conference on Education for All and the positive identification of many of them with the Education for All (EFA) Initiative, the NGOs referred to as EFA NGOs. In order to analyse the innovative quality of EFA NGO philosophy and practice in shifting the thinking around development, education and learning, the concept of open learning communities needs to be further defined.

While the process orientation of open learning communities counters the use of neat and precise definitions, it is possible to identify some notions which indicate the dynamic shift away from conventional notions around education and learning.

Following are some Notions of Open Learning Communities. The concept of open learning communities indicates shifts:

- — towards learning systems that are legitimized and defined by the communities concerned;
- — towards learning as tapping and building on local knowledge;
- — towards learning as a process of conscientization which involves discovering oneself and one's place in society;
- — towards radical community participation;
- — towards gender aware learning systems;
- — towards inter-generational learning;
- — towards a focus on learning to learn;
- — towards lifelong learning as a dynamic, interrelated process;
- — towards learning as relationship-building;
- — towards transcending the boundaries of formal, non-formal and informal education (beyond conventional institutionalized learning)
- — towards making multiple connections and practicing principles of learning organizations;
- — more to be added in the future.

The relations between the ideological dimensions of Jomtien, which are summarized in the Declaration on Education for All, and the notions of open learning communities as identified above shall be explored. When looking at the nature of the Declaration on Education for All we must bear in mind that it reflects a process of political compromise between the different stakeholders involved in education. Most EFA NGOs, for example, identify strongly with Article 2 of the Jomtien Declaration which stresses the need for unconventional approaches to education: "What is needed is an 'expanded vision' that surpasses present resource levels, institutional structures, curricula, and conventional delivery systems while building on the best of current practices."

Most governments, on the other hand, tend to particularly quote Article 5 of the Declaration which clearly explains that formal primary schooling is and should continue to be the basis for education systems, while non-formal programs are supposed to be supplementary: "The main delivery system for basic education of children outside the family is primary schooling.(...) . Supplementary alternative programs can help meet the basic learning needs of children with limited or no access to schooling, provided that they share the same standards of learning applied in schools ... "

In contrast, the concept of open learning communities calls for the radical questioning of the dominant position of formal standardized systems. Ideas around open learning communities suggest a shift towards a society with diverse learning systems which cut across age and time. The concept of open learning communities is not about rejecting or promoting existing approaches as such, but about actively reflecting and reconstructing them, which may or may not lead to a rejection or acceptance of conventional notions around education and learning.

An activity undertaken as part of the Education for All Initiative, e.g. an adult literacy program, may at the same time contribute to the construction of open learning communities. But the significance of this program will depend on the motivation and processes that lead to its set up and implementation. The Jomtien Declaration considers education, above all as a means to provide for and meet what is called a person's basic learning needs. These are said to comprise the need to acquire essential learning tools (such as literacy, oral expression, numeracy and problem solving) as well as learning content (such as knowledge, skills, values, and attitudes) required by human beings to be able to survive, to develop their full capacities,(...), and to continue learning.

Concepts of open learning communities dissociate themselves from the idea of knowledge transmission and advocate for learning as a social interactive creative process which releases human potential. Learning is perceived as a process of building relationships, giving meaning to the world, interrelating and constructing knowledge and entering into the world of meta-cognition.

The more functionalist notion of learning in the Education for All concept contrasts with the dynamic concept of learning within the context of open learning communities. The latter is more about facilitating and enabling processes rather than achieving definable results. There are many references in the Jomtien Declaration which reflect the notion that the learners and their communities are first and foremost perceived as having 'deficits'. The focus is on them as illiterates, not-life-skilled and not knowing numeracy.

In the context of open learning communities on the other hand, one starts from the assumption that there are in every learner and every community a multitude of knowledge systems and learning processes already operating which need to be tapped, nurtured and built upon. Learning is perceived as a process of linking the past, the present and the future. Both concepts talk about lifelong learning, but while in the context of Education for All the focus is on building on past knowledge, the thinking around open learning communities emphasizes continuous knowledge creation.

While the first refers to a more linear, gradual and step by step process, where separate learning needs are met one after another to eventually provide the "foundation of lifelong learning", the construction of open learning communities suggests a concept of learning which refers to multidimensional interrelated process that can not be broken down into neatly definable learning chunks, but rather releases human potential and the ability to create knowledge. The two concepts reflect the ideological traditions characterizing the educational and development discourse of their time.

While the Education for All concept as portrayed in the Jomtien Declaration primarily reflects notions of modern rational thinking and its concern with technical and economic progress, equal rights, autonomy and individual self fulfilment, the concept of open learning communities reflects notions of post modernist thinking. Post modernist thinking does not contradict modern thinking as such, but challenges the ways in which and on what grounds we perceive and organize the world including the underlying principles of the modernity paradigm.

It also reflects notions ot theories about lifelong learning and "learning to learn", feminist discourse, pluralism and radical pedagogy which will be discussed within the context of the following chapter. Ouane argues that many of the "new" ideas around education and learning, particularly the idea to shift towards integrated learning systems - i.e. overcoming the barriers of formal and non-formal education - are not only age old, but were also raised in Jomtien. Still, the follow-up process of the Conference has not been able to motivate a major shift to change the dominant education paradigm.

Since Jomtien, the main educational discourse continues to represent the perspective of formal schooling. The notions of open learning communities as presented above will provide a useful analytic tool.

Most EFA NGOs are involved in adult literacy programs. The introduction of a literacy program is often legitimized by emphasizing the positive impact of literacy for development. The illiteracy of the people is defined as a deficit which has to be overcome. However, this approach has often caused problems in that the literacy trainers, when starting their project, discover that the illiterates may not necessarily connect with their vision of development and do not share the external view that they are suffering from a deficit. They may reject the program.

Many EFA NGOs, when asked about their experiences in establishing literacy program, say that the hardest part of their work had been to get things started. "When going to the villages we realized that we did not really understand the people and their culture. In the beginning we did not know how to communicate our ideas to them. Only after we had established relationships with the people could we start discussing the issue with them.". Traditionally the next step in implementing the literacy program is the establishment of closer relations with the people in the community to convince them of the need for literacy. This often works and the literacy program can finally be established and may or may not result in valuable learning experiences for the community concerned.

However, the concept of open learning communities, suggests a slightly different approach. Rather than confronting a community with a fixed idea, the NGO would interact with the community to understand and raise awareness of existing communication structures and knowledge systems. The people themselves - with the assistance of the NGO - would engage in a continuous process of interaction and reflection on what development and learning means in their specific context to create their learning environment.

This process may or may not imply the setting up of a literacy program or other kinds of formal and/or non-formal programs. If it does, the meaning of these programs for the lives of the people will probably be different than a literacy program that was introduced by an external authority.

From the perspective of open learning communities, the introduction of any learning event in a community has to be legitimized by the community and should build on existing knowledge systems, communication structures and local institutions rather than be externally defined.

While a stimulus for joint reflection on learning can come from the outside, it is the concerned community which should be actively involved in constructing its learning environment. As one of the EFA NGO members interviewed said, "Community ownership evolves, it is not bestowed, granted or given by default".

Many EFA NGOs have been actively involved in developing and applying methodological tools to identify and reconstruct local knowledge systems and interactive learning structures. Maps, calendars, matrices, diagrams and other techniques have been used to raise awareness of the social dynamics of a community. One of the latest examples of a new methodological approach is the REFLECT Method developed by Action Aid.

In a REFLECT program there are no literacy textbooks, no pre-printed materials. The communities themselves develop their own learning materials that represent local dynamics, systematize the existing knowledge of learners and promote the analysis of local issues. The graphics become a permanent record for the community which can help it to further plan and negotiate its own development. These methodologies represent an important contribution to putting into practice notions of open learning communities and support a shift towards learning as tapping and building on local knowledge.

Many EFA NGO literacy programs have applied Freire's idea of generative themes and words. In this approach, a facilitator - ideally together with the community - identifies themes which are most central in the lives of the learners. These themes are discussed and put into writing with and gradually by the learners. Through the process of reading and writing the learners gain a distance from their day-to-day lives and rediscover and reconstruct the world and their places in it.

Open learning communities, just as radical pedagogy, is about conscientisation. Only if people are conscious of who they are, how they relate to others and what roles they play in society, can they actively participate in constructing open learning communities. The experience of EFA NGOs with these kinds of processes is very valuable to the construction of open learning communities.

Now the challenge remains to link this practice to other practices related to open learning communities. It is hard to find any EFA NGO which would reject the importance of community participation in community development. Different national NGOs and international NGOs, particularly Save the Children, have become involved in setting up community schools.

A closer look at the participatory aspect of these initiatives reveals that in these projects participation focuses on aspects of school financing, management and the recruitment of teachers from the community. Sometimes communities are also involved in decision-making on content and methodology, but in most cases it seems that the official school curriculum is used as the main reference point for curriculum development, though adapted to the community context.

Methodological and pedagogical issues are rarely developed with the community, which means that the potential value of local learning and indigenous knowledge systems remains largely untapped. Community participation is not practiced as a principle to facilitate the process of building a learning community, but is rather used as a tool to build an alternative school system for those who have no access to formal schooling. The ultimate role often tends to be the mainstreaming of children into formal schooling rather than building a community which allows its members to engage in collaborative interactive and inter-generational lifelong learning.

Community education approaches have a lot to contribute to the discourse on community participation. Several EFA NGOs follow approaches which fall under the broad category of community education. The International Community Education Association (ICEA) with its regional branches all over the world has been playing a key role in further researching and developing the concept.

According to the ICEA, community education involves a holistic approach which supports learning in, with and for the community. The objective is to enable the community to solve social, cultural, technological, economic and ecological problems and thereby foster integrated development. Freire's technique of identifying generative themes is used to define the problems of the communities. Community education tries to provide an answer to specific weaknesses of institutions and curricula in the formal system.

Examples of community education practice comprise a great variety of activities ranging from projects on alternative tourism with out-of school youth, theatre projects with the homeless, deforestation projects, cross-community interaction programs in areas of conflict or income-generating activities. Most of the community education programs seem to focus on one particular group which are referred to as the marginalized and aim at creating spaces for them within the larger community.

In the context of open learning communities, gender aware learning systems would be systems that consciously reflect and build on the gender dynamics in a community. The relationships between women and men and the different roles they play in their communities would be analysed by the community concerned to identify in how far gender specific knowledge and ways of learning exist and why.

Some EFA NGOs already move in this direction by integrating gender as one of the themes in their literacy programs. The learners individually and collectively gain a new understanding about their roles and place in the community in relation to the other sex. This process is the beginning of reconstructing and redefining gender relations. Since most societies today are characterized by patriarchal structures, gender awareness training which forms part of many adult education programs, has become an important tool for women's empowerment.

The concept of open learning communities suggests to involve both women and men in reflecting on existing gender dynamics. More research needs to be done on how this joint reflection can be facilitated. Gender conscientisation is particularly interesting in the context of open learning communities, since it provides a tool to reveal what kind of gender specific learning processes, knowledge and learning systems can be found in a learning community and how these can be accounted for and built upon. A deeper analysis of what specific women's education programs carried out by EFA NGOs, can contribute to the construction of open learning communities, has yet to be done.

In creating community education centers with specific activities for parents, they try to narrow the growing gap between children and their parents. Family literacy programs present another attempt of NGOs to promote inter-generational learning. Children and parents organize learning as an interactive process. The concept of open learning communities would take the notion of inter-generational learning a step further and interpret it as a process of rediscovering and re-establishing inter-generational community dynamics to strengthen dialoguing between and among the different generations.

While EFA NGOs do emphasize the importance of "learning to learn", it is hard to find research which examines NGO activity in this field in more depth. However one example is the Boithuto, Seliba Sa - Center for Self-Study is a project that was developed as an attempt to respond to the question of how the responsibility for learning can be given back to the learner. A wide variety of learners from different age groups come to the Center whenever and how often they want.

Linking formal and non-formal education has been a major issue for EFA NGOs. Many argue that the formal system could benefit from the methods and experiences of the non-formal sector which they consider to be more flexible and dynamic in responding to the learning needs of a rapidly changing world. The metaphor often heard to illustrate the relation between the two is that of a bridge.

The use of the term bridge indicates that while some connections can be made, the autonomy of the two systems is not questioned. If for example a non-formal program is successful in preparing a learner to finally enter the formal system, the term bridging is used. Open learning communities would take the notion a step further. Rather than using the metaphor of a bridge the concept would suggest multiple connections between the systems which would constitute a new structure or a new whole.

Most EFA NGOs define their role as complementary to that of the government and the formal system. According to this logic, a radical shift beyond the existence of three separate systems does not seem urgent. Though the Jomtien declaration calls for surpassing present institutional structures and delivery systems, the Jomtien process does not seem to have been able to motivate this radical shift.

Collaborative structures and networks can be found at the national, regional and international levels. The intention is to explore in how far the existing networks can be considered examples of open learning communities and, as such, partners in further contributing to the process of developing shared visions and practices of open learning communities.

Professionalization in this sense would mean developing more professional self-confidence and integrity on the part of the NGO in negotiations and communication with communities, governments, funding agencies and international organizations. It should not prevent NGOs from, but encourage them to question the current practices in education by trying to 'see' and 'do' things differently and experiment with innovative ideas. Going beyond the status quo is a major concern of open learning communities, particularly in view of the rapid changes in the world today and the manifold crisis we are witnessing. If the CC wants to be innovative it may be worthwhile to take some time and collectively reflect on what development means to the individual members and in how far that responds to their approach to learning.

The value of the capacity building activities carried out within the framework of the Collective Consultation for the process of constructing and putting into practice individual and shared visions of learning and development will depend on the nature and content of the activities. It will be desirable to tap and build on the unique qualities and experiences of each NGO involved in order to nurture the diversity there is, while at the same time linking it with experiences of others as well as with latest insights gained in areas of concern to open learning communities, such as learning to learn, the use of traditional and modern technology, gender analysis, local knowledge systems and communication patterns, linguistic and cultural diversity and others.

Several NGOs explained that close cooperation with the Government in the field of non-formal education has often led to a situation where the NGO was expected to adapt its approach to the educational objectives of the governments rather than to its own priorities. On the other hand, according to some members of the Collective Consultation, close cooperation with governments has also led to mutual learning processes. One such example is Senegal where the government is involving NGOs with experience in non-formal education programs in formulating the country's plan for girls and women's education and in teacher training activities.

In order to evaluate the impact of government-NGO relationships, their substance and quality has to be carefully assessed. One example of a comprehensive study on government-NGO relations in basic education was carried out in Pakistan. Without being able to elaborate on the findings in any detail here, the results show that generalizations are difficult to make within one country. Relations vary according to region and often according to the absence or existence of functioning personal relations between an NGO member and a government.

The Education for All Network was established a few months after the World Conference on Education for All in 1990 calling on all partners to join their efforts to achieve the goal of Education for All by the year 2000. To establish a mechanism which would ensure NGO involvement in the process, NGOs initiated an interagency network of NGOs, United Nations agencies, universities and other education related institutions and networks committed to promoting Education for All.

The network was to focus its activities at national and regional levels to assist and encourage NGOs to actively participate in the EFA follow up. Thus far, four regional networks have been established with NGO membership. While the national NGO networks are showing increasing interest in the field of professional capacity building related to literacy and lifelong learning, the originally focused on expanding management capacities. The assumption was that strengthened institutional and management skills would have a beneficial impact on development policies and wider political processes.

The main emphasis for NGOs involved in such efforts is usually held to be the "process" involved in supporting local initiative rather than "content." The members of the EFA Network and the CC are also linked to other networks which are influential in defining and putting into practice ideas and concepts which fall under the broad category of non-formal education.

Two examples of networks linked with the CC which focus on adult learning and community education are the International Council on Adult Education (ICAE) and the International Community Education Association (ICEA) which emphasize their ideological links with ideas of radical pedagogy as discussed above. As long as these networks do not compete, but rather connect and collaborate, they can be considered important potential partners in thinking and further conceptualizing open learning communities. They can play a crucial role in supporting a shift towards new ways of looking at learning and development, but also in putting the concept into practice.

Inspiring the process of constructing individual and shared visions of open learning communities is about getting as many people involved as possible. The process calls for open communication structures which need the support of a world wide web of learning. It chose to analyse EFA NGOs as a potential inspiring force and confronted their philosophy and practice with some notions indicating the shifts toward the dynamic process of constructing open learning communities, making a continuous effort to rethink roles, philosophies and practices in learning and development. Several areas of activities were identified where EFA NGOs engage in practices going beyond conventional educational approaches, particularly in the fields of literacy, adult and community education.

They open their programs to different age groups, experiment with approaches which are more context specific, take into account and support cultural and linguistic diversity, and they link learning to other areas such as health, income-generation or agriculture. By designing context specific programs they try to meet the learners where they are and develop the learning materials accordingly. Many have recognized the political dimension of education and draw heavily from Freire's ideas of radical pedagogy.

Several have gained experiences in facilitating community participation and are concerned about the reconstruction of local knowledge systems. In doing so, the programs are geared towards facilitating processes of empowerment on the part of the learners and their communities. All these activities indicate the potential to promote the construction of open learning communities in that they try to move towards a culture of active learning rather than one centered around knowledge transmission.

However, in many cases the practices focus on one specific group in a community or one isolated 'problem' neglecting the concern of open learning communities to tap and build on a community's potential, knowledge systems, communication patterns and learning processes in a comprehensive manner, nurturing the growing of the whole rather than only its individual parts. Most EFA NGOs tend to stay and act in non-formal education and experiment within that protected space.

Some examples of attempts to link the separate systems of formal and non-formal education were identified, but they do not indicate a major shift towards contributing to the construction of a holistic and interlinked system. Similarly, joint policy statements made by EFA NGOs at international level are modest in advocating the transcendence of existing separate systems; rather they emphasize their complementarity. They also emphasize the complementarity of NGO and government roles in education with the former being the main actor in the non-formal sphere and the latter in the formal which, as the paper discussed, depending on the quality and degree of trust on both sides can be both conducive to, but sometimes also hindering the process towards constructing open learning communities.

The chances and limitations of NGO activity and their critical and innovative potential was discussed within the context of their growing role as implementing agencies for governments and donors. In how far vested interest rather than commitment lead an NGO's activities is a question that each NGO and indeed all actors involved in education, have to continuously asked themselves.

NGO networking and their attempts to link their organizations and activities and engage in collaborative reflection and action to further develop the quality of their involvement in education. These efforts are in support of the concern of open learning communities to create shared visions of lifelong learning.

The overall impact of these growing world wide webs of learning on the construction of open learning communities will largely depend on the interest of their members to consider issues critical to promoting shifts in conventional discourse and practice on education and development.

Many of the innovative ideas of EFA NGOs go back to the 1970s and 1980s. In view of the rapidly changing world of the 1990s, the complex crisis of leadership, institutions and meaning as well as new insights we have gained about how we learn. EFA NGOs may want to take some time to jointly reconsider their understanding of development and how it relates to learning. This reflection would be part of the process of sharing individual and joint visions around learning and development.

The existing networks may also consider opening their spaces of joint reflection to other actors involved in learning and development including official authorities. If NGOs wish to transcend conventional discourse and practice in education on a broader scale, this dialogue which is already happening in some cases, is important in a process of moving toward shared visions among all those involved in education and development.

The different networks or learning communities of EFA NGOs are constantly struggling to represent the diversity of NGOs involved in education, including grassroots movements and associations.

There are still many NGOs excluded from the collective thinking process, which reinforces ruptures between the local and the global discussion rather then linkages. Joint capacity building activities provide one opportunity to inspire collective thinking and action, but what other tools and structures can be used or developed to engage the diversity of NGOs in the process of creating visions of open learning communities?

Many grassroots movements or NGOs are experimenting with different ways of learning, but their experiences remain largely unknown. The flow of information from the grassroots to the national and international levels or from the periphery to the center is often blocked.

The starting point of information highways is currently the geographic or intellectual North. Much remains to be explored about the relations between current NGO practices in the field of women's education on the one hand and gender approaches on the other. Exploring these relations may also contribute to further conceptualizing open learning communities. While EFA NGOs can to some extent be considered to be among those inspiring the process of constructing open learning communities.

Transforming Community Schools into Open Learning Communities

During 1970s, International Community Education Association (ICEA) which was founded, whose goal is to promote the concept of Community Education and help form a working network of worldwide initiatives. Today ICEA is represented in some 90 countries, accredited by the Council of Europe, and has operational relations with UNESCO. Community Education stands for learning in the community, with the community, and for the community. It is to be understood as an integrating element of urban, community, and regional development efforts, contributing to the construction and reconstruction of economic infrastructure, cultural vitality and diversity, ecological consciousness and structural forms.

Community Education serves to expand individual and communal responsibility aimed at taking action for the improvement in the quality of life. Hence Community Education means interventional learning in the Polis, and assumes that learning persons are also active social, economical, ecological, and political beings.

The relationship between teachers and learners becomes a different one. Possibilities for an education towards entrepreneurship arise here, allowing people to take economic initiatives instead of only referring them to the nonexistent aid from agents of conventional control.

Orientation towards the community, opening places of learning to the social environment, understanding the learning process as a part of local development, the connection between learning and community development in general: Community Education is not "pedagogy" in the classical sense, but rather an active discourse and participation in complex realities. The idea of Community Education has many years of broad practical experience behind it. But the knowledge gained could hitherto hardly be made available for scholarly systematization and theoretical development.

Key problems such as the process of empowerment or ethnically strong communities in their struggles with the conflict between tradition and modernization have up to now been too little considered in the light of Community Education. However this does not change the fact that exactly these topics are those that have proven to be crucial in practice, as well as providing a focus in the theoretical development of innovative pedagogy and the comprehension of psychosocial processes.

Community Education has taken diverse forms worldwide, with reference to different sources in the history of thought. The practical models of progressive education in USA and the Community Schools of Educational Priority Areas in England were committed to the philosophy of Community Education; principles of Community Education can be recognized in the public education movement in Korea at the time of the Japanese occupation, in popular education emerging from the anti-apartheid movement in South Africa; today such currents are to be found in the Economía Popular and further developed Education Popular in Latin America as well as the Buddhist-influenced Productive Community Schools in Thailand, Islamic oriented Pesantren in Indonesia or the Youth at Risk projects or Neighbourhood Schools in Europe.

The opportunities offered by Community Education to relate learning processes directly to actual problems in real-life situations, and thereby combine reflection and action with each other in a meaningful way, often harbour certain dangers, considering the overall contextual constraints which Community Education has to deal with, especially in the socioeconomic peripheral regions. Curtailment in practice is one danger. Others include programs dominated by conventional pedagogical measures (such as a frontal classroom for illiterates), as well as whole institutions which serve more as retreats for pedagogues escaping reality than as point of departure for engaging pedagogical activity in unprotected terrain, can also turn into aberrations on the educational landscape. There is neither a universal definition nor a well-developed theory of Community Education.

On the contrary, the analysis of the diverse developmental directions of this approach, its theoretical references and practical implementations, demonstrate that there is a kind of agreement on a number of central principles which form the basis for a pedagogical, educational, and sociopolitical orientation of Community Education and for the design of life and learning processes. Such principles include for instance a holistic approach, life-long learning, empowerment, participation, help towards self-help, community development, decentralization, the networking of different areas of life and learning as well as of institutions and resources, and a cross-generational, multi-topical, interdisciplinary cooperation and partnership.

The demand for Community Education is growing worldwide. This quantitative development has brought with it a large store of on-site experience. Characteristic of the hitherto weak infrastructure of the movement, however, is the lack of comparative culturally sensitive documentation and archiving of such experiences. Related to this fact is the concomitant lack of theoretical development on the phenomenon.

The theory deficit on the one hand and the diverse, often undesired limitation of Community Education on the other hand make it clear that Community Education is a concept that needs to be elucidated, as Cyril Poster already pointed out in 1982. Particularly problematical and needful of clarification is the term "community".

By nature, Community Education crosses borders. For educators and pedagogical scientists, this invaluable access to reality provides a largely yet unprocessed challenge. Community Education deals with de-schooled learning, which can certainly be promoted when institutions of the formal educational system become more open to the outside world. Nevertheless, contradictions between educational processes more strongly subjected to didactic reduction, and learning and experiencing procedures in the sense of Community Education, are in fact part of the educational landscape of many countries.

Community education is not easy to introduce, since it challenges existing professional and administrative hierarchies and cuts right across the different domains. In its developmental stage it is not a panacea for all ills but may even add to the complexity of social development processes and procedures. Yet, once beyond this developmental stage, when it has demonstrated its principles and shown its implementation possibilities, its rationale becomes clear and leads to the realization of its aims and objectives.

The following distinguishing features of Community Education emerge as important:

— Community education is a holistic approach which supports the learning in, with and for the community. It counts on self-reliance, mobilizes the power of communities and focuses them on sustainable development, on the solution of social, cultural, technological, economic and ecological problems. All the social and all the age groups of the population can be involved. That is why community education overcomes the separatism of "hyphen-pedagogies", when the project allows it; it is more than just adult education or vocational training. It works in an integrating way.

— The key problems and situations of the people in the community are the starting point of the learning process. As generative themes in the sense expressed by Paulo Freire, many of these problems and situations have more than just a local meaning, they also contain supra-regionally relevant parts. The search for local alternative forms of energy can become a contribution to prevent global climatic changes. Many local problems (with their global aspects) cannot be solved without the supporting approach or community education. This is true for family planning just as much as for dealing with our natural resources in a responsible way.

— Community education is never just education, but always organization and action as well. Thus the application of acquired knowledge and abilities in complex real-life situations becomes an integral part of the learning process. Not only is the subject the point of concentration, but also the situation that should be dealt with and improved. That is why community education never just aims at the qualification of people, but also at a constructive dealing with the reality in which these people are living.

— Community education is especially sensitive and responsible with regard to the living conditions of marginalized ethnic groups. It supports social movements that aim at overcoming this marginalization. It makes an effort for full equal rights of women. It promotes the realization of human rights, the integration and acceptance of ethnic, cultural or religious minorities, it has an intercultural and antiracist orientation. It becomes active against the isolation of handicapped people.

— Community Education and popular economics work together in many cases. From the beginning ICEA has seen and emphasized the importance of economics from below as a way out of marginalization. Here ICEA above all emphasizes the promotion of entrepreneurship. For where there is a lack of jobs, people have to be able to create jobs themselves. ICEA supports those, often from the informal sector, who want to get access to the regular market.

— Community education is an answer to specific weaknesses of institutions and curricula in the formal educational sector. Learning as participation in sustained development does not need any artificial motivation. It is easier to put new insights into reality. Academic knowledge is used for concrete problems and not taught in an alienated form. Knowledge and abilities can be acquired in a process of investigating learning with a close connection of theory and practice.

— Community schools are referring to local needs with their curriculum, they reconstruct the relationship to the neighbourhood and lead children and adolescents at an early point and more intensively than traditional schools to social fields of action. This also outlines the paradigm of community education in contrast to conventional educational approaches:

— Learning processes are not cut up into meaningless units and placed beyond reality. Community education lays emphasis on holistic learning in meaningful connections. Technical qualifications with instruments are learnt in an enlightened social context. Learning does not take place in parameters of phony security where tasks, the method of solving the problem and the solution are all known beforehand. Instead, learning takes place in the uncertainty of complex reality. People learn in a close theory-practice correlation. Community education favours the inquiring and discovering type of learning -learning through productive action.

— Community education emphasizes development of the curriculum from the bottom up instead of the top down. Subjects do not structure it but key situations and key problems. Their analysis makes the classification of desirable qualifications possible which allow autonomous, competent action and solidarity. The connection with key situations initiates learning processes close to reality and a focus of scientific knowledge on real problems.

— Community education contributes to an opening of educational institutions to social action fields without being fixed to educational institutions. Here it is accepted that important social learning processes take place - especially under conditions of marginalization -beyond the walls of educational institutions.

— Community educators are not shaped by white-collar convictions, they do not migrate from the land and they do not rely on teacher-proof curricula. They interpret learning as an active participation in local and regional development. They combine brain-work with manual work.

Open Learning Community would mistake their role if they did not become critical and simultaneously constructive adversary of only pragmatic variants of Community Education; the development of standards of excellence is necessary right there, where due to their existential situation, people cannot afford to grind through an examination-ridden curriculum alienated from reality.

Community Schools promote cross-generational learning in many project forms. Looking around in the classrooms in the morning, one can find housewives, unemployed people, and workers in their free shift, all who join the young people there studying for their O or A-levels in Geography or Physics. In the evenings and on weekends one finds young people and adults alike, attending classes together in computer technology, law, or auto repair, or pursuing common hobbies such as body building and yoga.

Tolerance is the prerequisite for the British variant of Community Education. Nothing is smoothed over here, no special paths paved; everyone is admitted, and if need be the matter is discussed. Hence old women and men practicing folkdances meet up with punkers who are going to a karate class.

Women in their mid-40's are putting on a Beauty Salon event while teachers and students are out blocking a railway track to stop a train loaded with weapons, as part of a protest campaign "Schools against the bomb". Youngsters quarrel with British foreign policy, while Oldies stand at the bar and recapitulate the bleak situation of the Argentinean soldiers on the Falkland Islands, while sipping their sherry.

Open learning, open planning, a less cramped, less formalized relationship with each other and topics of study that are not only subordinate to academic subjects, but having something to do with real life going on all around them - something to do with the lousy, boring, poor, rich, small-people-life of ordinary folk, with their chichi and knickknacks, unemployment and garden plots, with the fight against bureaucratic windmills, with the Gala evening and fancy supper and Offenbach the Ratby Brass Band in the gym.

Students and teachers as communal politicians: the unemployment in the community of Groby is reflected in the self-help programs of the school. Hence right next to the picturesque, right next to Ann Brown's Cake

Decoration, an initiative group is trying to counteract the hopelessness of unemployed youth and adults in ever getting a job on the regular marketplace by founding their own small enterprise. Here is a school which also acts as a place where the despairing can find comfort, and the discouraged can join together to do something about their lot.

Sometimes teachers at Community Schools risk having to be pastor, therapist, and rebel all in one. Opening schools means in Great Britain: including parents and other adults in the school's daily life, and not only pushing them out of the way into powerless committees; not treating people from the neighbourhood as foreigners in the school environment; making the school into a city centre; making learning also possible beyond the school's walls, where people live and work.

A Community Relations Council assumes many administrative tasks that would otherwise fall to the school principal: this self-governing organ consisting of parents, teachers, and representatives from associations and communal government coordinates the activities of the school. Teachers are not only teachers. In Bradford some of them are partly freed to work as home liaison teachers and visit pubs, companies, businesses, temples, and homes, to talk with people, to find out their needs, and to report back their experience to the school and see to it that the school reacts appropriately with an adequate offer.

Although in England of the early 80's the subject-related final exams were largely standardized, the ways to achieving this goal were not. Pedagogical freedom in this case consists of the ability to break up the standard timetable and develop one's own curriculum. An ossified principal can block developments at this schools for years on end, but the head of a Community School is not permitted (and would not want) to pull the brakes on development by constantly imposing practical restraints and administrative regulations from above.

In every community there are people which can teach something of value to others. A Community School is a popular facility - one can win elections with it. Such a school is cost efficient. It helps in the development of social infrastructure, supports neighbourly relations and self-reliance.

A Community school does not alienate people as much as other schools, or as one of the teachers in Quran expressed it: ever since they had such a school, there has been no more vandalism, windowpanes were not broken "when the school happened to be closed ". A school in Nürnberg titled a public function during the 80's "Open up the schools and let life in". When one talks with school principals in Europe about the possibilities of reducing the daycare character of schools and opening them up to their neighbourhoods and communities, one finds many who are for the idea and many that are also despondent.

Learning and Earning

Poor children cannot afford childhood. Millions of them live on the street and care for themselves, sleeping in doorways or under bushes. They work on their own accounts or illegally in factories. They cope with corrupt police and know how to sweet-talk customers. They help each other and pay protection money. They form gangs and hunt for prey. They perform self-justice and have pity. They develop their own toys. They sell bananas and drugs, newspapers and chiclets; they harvest cotton, clean shoes, and carry rocks. Life for them is filled with risk, for they could die of parasites, beatings, or starvation. Yet at the same time it is replete with adventure, better than the grimmest hut that can never be a home or the dull prison of welfare. The children of the Third World are more capable than the children of invented childhood.

Productive Community Schools could mean 1000 colourful flowers, 1000 variations and attempts to acquire extensive experience through the realization that school should not cause the children of the poor to lose their entrepreneurial skills. Instead it should start at the point they have already reached on their own.

The International Community Education Association has provided 5000 dollars of start-up funds for both schools. The Bumaka School set up a forestry school and a swimming-pool-sized tank for fish-breeding and began raising cattle. Two years after its establishment the forestry school is already profitable; the cattle herd has already doubled in size, and the cattle-raising enterprise remains profitable despite the fall in beef prices. Only the fish nursery is bringing in less cash because most of the fish are eaten in the mornings by the students. The Bumaka teachers strove with success to pay the invested money as quickly as possible into a revolving fund and to start up additional projects.

In the process they at first tried to avoid paying the students. Soon enough, though, they learned that student-entrepreneurs also need economic incentives in order to keep enthusiasm alive. The Gudbost School did not have these start-up problems. It concentrates on chicken-breeding, and after four production cycles (four generations of chickens) it had not only recouped its initial investments, but even earned enough capital to set up a forestry school.

New teaching materials are being drawn up and sold to other schools. The primers are no longer called "reading," "writing," and "arithmetic," but rather "fish breeding," "cattle raising," and "forestry," and they contain a great deal about the how and why of business.

The term "Community School" than simply a school run by the community, then such a school must be characterized in all its institutionalized and differing variations by the following features:

— It combines global and local concerns in its curriculum, and a part of the curriculum refers to local key problems. It takes advantage of the freedom and flexibility granted by the curriculum, expands and interprets it with the goal of penetrating the immediate vicinity, deciphering the large universe by understanding the small one next door, and joining reflection with concrete action - here and not just someplace.

— It integrates school and adult education; school classes and adult education work both take place on Community School premises, functioning together with regard to content and context. Adults are also welcome as students in the morning classes as well. In the afternoon and evenings, age-specific and mixed age activities and courses are offered.

Such a school is directed at people of different ages, at families, at neighbours. The school puts its available resources (workshops, specialty rooms, sports facilities, classrooms, kitchen, library, etc.) at the disposal of its new clientele. The physical school has multiple functions, and not only on weekends. The school is not there only as a learning venue, but also as a cultural and leisure time facility. Associations and initiative groups can meet there, and a good part of the extracurricular activities are for pleasure.

It is a basis for self-help: for neighbours as well as unemployed youths, for people who wish to qualify themselves in certain fields as well as for those who are looking for human contact, since they aren't getting anywhere with their problems on their own.

A Community School networks with other external learning venues, builds satellites, works on projects with other non-school groups and institutions. It works against segregation, and against the splitting of young and old, domestic and foreign, handicapped and non-handicapped, inner life and outer world. Its teachers are not only teachers but also community developers.

Important chances of retaining the relationship between schools and community were simply gambled away, and the potential uses of schools as learning and experiencing centres on a larger scale basically ignored. Right up until his death, the Italian psychiatrist Franco Basaglia headed a movement for getting rid of psychiatric hospitals, and he left an inheritance which certainly does not sit well with Italians. His sociologist wife Franca Ongara Basaglia, once reproached international pedagogues with behaving no better than psychiatrists. They branded their clientele with the label "immature", isolated them off in large institutions, and then claimed that this practice was a particularly good preparation for maturity and life.

They tended to build ever more institutes and train ever more specialists in the effort to constantly increase their professional influence. They lived off the inner conflict between the exclusion and re-integration of their clientele. This is a good observation, but it by no means suffices to lead to practicable alternatives - just think of the de-schooling discussion sparked by Ivan Illich some two dozen years ago, and its quiet demise in pedagogical salons.

For more and more people, such institutions have become their familiar habitat for ever longer periods. The quantitative extension of pedagogical institutions has not only allowed more advancement, but has also become a new characteristic of depository safekeeping and the long march through even more institutions.

A part of this school phenomenon, especially in industrialized countries, is the tendency towards compression and multiple parallel classes. Hence the centrally located school "conveniently situated", meaning: a school district delivering children from within a 20 kilometer radius; or the huge school complex with 10 parallel classes for each grade, resulting from the argument that only thus can differentiated courses be offered and optimal facilities afforded.

Schools as huge blocks, distributed throughout the country according to the criteria of some centralized school development plan, often monumental in size, and frequently without an inkling of the notion that pedagogy begins to curdle into mere administrative activity under certain conditions, and that perfect facilities can destroy pedagogical improvisation and fantasy.

Another aspect is the tendency towards the increase and constant change of teachers - the fact that it has become unusual that pedagogues remain with children for longer periods of time or even over a number of years. In a rhythm of early and late shifts, in hourly intervals, separated into half or full years, the children are treated for a while and then passed on. It has become rare that the next colleague can or even wants to ask the previous one about the life history, interests, qualifications and needs of the children.

This complicated mechanism, patched together with substitute and temporary teachers, does not lead to mobility, as Hellmut Becker called for at the beginning of the west German educational reform movement, but rather to alienation, to a kind of "hospitalism" concealed as simple lack of motivation, to a materialism of thought on the part of educational administrators, kindergarten workers, teachers, and students who are not capable of even imagining it all any differently.

Safekeeping and restacking requires the expansion of the peer group principle right down to the day nursery, and the perfecting of forms for external differentiation, beginning with separation into three or four different performance levels per subject and culminating in the network of main subjects, optional and obligatory subjects, advanced and basic courses.

If a teacher had the spontaneous idea of developing a project out of an actual situation and it could not be completed within the 50 minutes at his disposal, further class connections would be endangered and the entire distribution modus of teachers and students would begin to topple.

The quantitative extension of the education system must satisfy the right of gaining knowledge more than ever. Day care centers are necessary when both parents work. Children are to be stimulated in kindergarten. The principle of birth year as primary grouping criterion is practical. The subject teacher is generally more competent than the village teacher.

Changing inwardly means breaking through rigid rituals, creating clear connections and contexts, and ongoing relationships between children and teachers, replacing an external differentiation with an internal one, opening up the frontal classroom structure by increasingly favoring project-oriented teaching, making school facilities more hospitable - after all, here is the living space of children and young people for many years.

And opening outwards means including parents in pedagogical daily life, and not just in committee work, treating people from the neighborhood as partners and not strangers, viewing schools as community and regional centers where children and young people can take part in local and regional developments. Our communities, cities, and landscapes are imperfect enough, contain enough that is contradictory, that we can learn from them and deal with their realities on a reduced scale.

The purely subject-oriented curriculum proves to operate as fetters especially where there are strong centralized government controls - particularly when teachers are made executors of a catalog of subject matter by a swift succession of centrally regulated and often centrally evaluated tests and exams - subject matter which they must attempt to teach in a specifically tailored form and style of repetitive learning.

The contents of such curricula, including the textbooks used, often have very little or nothing at all to do with the local reality. They are not set up to transfer what has been learned, but instead form an almost closed circle, within which the pupils can move forward only with the help of extrinsic motivating steam.

But even where curricula are somewhat more flexible and open, most teachers apparently find it difficult to organize the subject matter away from rigid categories and disciplines in some new manner, to focus them on real problems and to approach such problems with the students in a practical way. This difficulty is illustrated by the example of the private Hermann Lietz-Schule on the Baltic Sea island Spiekeroog, founded in the 1920's during the sweep of educational forms of the time, which faced an almost total collapse in the 80's.

The school had to act entrepreneurially, and now students suddenly became important - the school depended on them for its survival. Soon the students were saying that they could surround the school (which was already a non-profit limited-liability company) with additional small companies, transform classes into small enterprises, plunder the material from morning classes and incorporate knowledge useful for their companies into their projects.

The students could design small solar-power vehicles for use on the island (where automobiles are banned). Or they could create all-terrain vehicles with rollers and caterpillar tracks for vacationing families whose strollers would normally sink in the sand on the way through the dunes. Or the school could open a cafe for visitors returning hungry and thirsty from the seaside.

The old subjects should continue to be offered, albeit in reduced form. The truly important knowledge could be acquired more effectively in the small companies beyond the 50-minute rhythm of the class day. Then they would learn for real. After all, anyone who wants to cultivate one or two hectares of agricultural land under glass roofs rather than scraping frozen vegetables from the land in winter needs considerable prior knowledge in the areas of management, geography, biology, chemistry, physics, and mathematics.

Curriculum committees are not omniscient. Curricula contain nothing about the best way, under the conditions prevailing in Spiekeroog, to produce soil which not only contains nutrients but also retains water thanks to admixtures of clay. But the islanders know. Their help and their expertise should be used to avoid failures. Plans were made, discussed, discarded - and yet much was done as well.

Teaching staff, school directors, and school supervisors have to share a common interest in developing a school in the direction of a Community School. An active minority among the teachers wanting to convince a sluggish majority of the new idea can easily wear itself down in the process, before the school develops a certain profile.

Even a generally motivated teaching staff can quickly lose its staying power when a Community School merely means more work, when increased commitment is not connected with incentives, and financial, structural, and personnel support is not forthcoming. In countries where teachers generally have to hold down second and even third jobs to supplement their frugal teaching salary, such additional skills and experiences are generally not considered a useful resource for the school.

The two spheres remain totally separated: in the morning a teacher in Brazilian Porto Alegre stands in front of the class and adheres to a strict syllabus, and in the afternoon the same person is a risk-taker, namely a chicken breeder and survival artist.

Whereas the school acts like a magnet on some teachers, constantly drawing them in and quickly blocking any excursions out beyond the school walls, there are other teachers who naturally dedicate themselves with heart and soul to social and enterprising activity, who favor an open and project-oriented kind of teaching, and who sincerely endeavor to reshape the relationship between school and neighborhood.

Whoever wants to transform existing schools into Community Schools is well advised to advertise the planned "profile schools" and give teachers inclined for such work the chance of applying forpositions there, while at the same time providing an opportunity for current teachers skeptical to the idea to apply for a teaching post elsewhere.

One can impute that in some countries those responsible for educational policy harbor relative ignorance about what a fully developed concept of a Community School looks like and what kind of political sense the introduction of Community Schools makes for young people. The entire concept of Community Education is unknown in not just a few countries, and portions of the concept go under other names.

In those places where Community Schools are supported by official educational policy and achieve increasing impetus, the following reasons for the political relevance of this type of school are mentioned.

Community Schools can counteract and cut down the alienation at school experienced by so many children and adolescents. This applies to families and neighbors as well, especially in multicultural school districts Community Schools can function as urban and community centers and make significant contributions to social and infrastructural development by promoting good neighborly relations and self-reliance.

Cost-benefit analyses demonstrate that a Community School with the outlined integrated functions works considerably more cheaply than separate facilities. Interest is growing in those countries or regions in which enlightened policy has provided experience with this type of school - it grows, because Community Schools have proved to be particularly suited to address social problems and develop practical contributions to their solution.

Community Schools can counteract violence and vandalism. They can serve to develop a social network, promote meaningful activity and support the formation of a school community. Real-life problems are not kept out of the underlying syllabus, but consciously confronted. Cross-generational experiences are promoted through joint projects which work against isolation and loneliness.

Students and adults participate in creating the program and increasingly experience that their affairs are dealt with in the school and neighborhood. When young people translate their socioeconomic marginalization into racism, it becomes necessary to attack the underlying problem with an increased intercultural educational process: the Community School on the one hand as a place which can have natural multicultural characteristics and experienced as cultural enriching; on the other hand as basis for self-help, as a facility where one learns to search for paths leading out of social seclusion.

Job-oriented education is often limited to the promotion of employee qualifications. When there is a great deal of unemployment or the threat of unemployment, however - as in for example former socialist countries today - and there is a historically caused, understandable lack of entrepreneurial initiative in the population, it becomes especially important to support and promote entrepreneurial qualities and hence increase the chances of school graduates creating jobs for themselves and not becoming passive victims of a weak job market. This type of entrepreneur from below, full of ideas and almost obsessed with getting ahead, capable of long-term strategic behavior and equipped with social and ecological consciousness, has barely been noted by the pedagogical world.

Community Schools have already gathered quite a bit of experience (as Productive Community Schools; with the founding of spin-off companies and small enterprises), which indicate that entrepreneurship is a lot more and a lot different than simply the teaching of professional skills in Business Administration, and that a certain entrepreneurial initiative and professionalism can be promoted at school.

The tendency noticeable in some countries to distribute central federal competencies more than before to the regions, especially to the municipality, places the citoyen more into the limelight as one who acts as a corrective to the old-time political guild and makes and extends his own political sphere of action himself. In this context a neighborhood school is not only a school as

Polis, but also a school in the Polis - it allows for interventional learning and participates in the politics of the immediate area.

A politically competent and differentiated support of the development of Community Schools is an exception the world over. In reality, uninformed opinions generally dominate on the political level, taking the "classic" educational reform countries such as Great Britain, the USA, Canada, or Australia. This fact does not exclude the existence of first-rate individual Community Schools which have come into being because teachers, concerned people in school supervision, or dedicated parents have seriously committed themselves to the concept.

Where the opening of schools to the community has at least become a part of the educational policy program, there is often a contradiction between the relatively broad consensus on the importance of Community Schools and the only modest implementation of the idea in practice. Hence it is important for educational policy to primarily concentrate at the local level on the clarification and realization of a structural, conceptual, and financial framework for the operation of Community Schools.

An Open Learning Community is a broad concept embracing a network of groups and institutions which come together for a certain purpose, pursue a common goal, and attain knowledge in the process. There are plenty of cases in which this has occurred without the participation of either pedagogues or money-providing institutions to trigger the process.

An Open Learning Community does not automatically arise because people and institutions have been stimulated to work and learn together as much as possible. A generative topic is needed, some issue that truly touches people in their own lives. A problem cannot be artificially "planted", it must be either latently or manifestly present. In joint learning processes, in combining reflection with action, the chance has to be recognized and grasped to develop strategies for problem solving that involve intervening in situations to work for the improvement of those involved.

A situation and problem analysis of some sort is necessary, carried out in discussion with those affected. A theory or approach to the situation or problem must be developed, in order to begin applying attempted solutions at strategic points. There are a whole series of possible methods which can be used in clarifying the relationships involved.

The generative core stimulates the learning and development process when it represents an actual problem complex consciously recognized by someone involved. It generates goals, activities, and mutual duties of those learning. This analysis completes a "participatory research", in which in principal all those participating in a situation can be involved. Such research is to be equated with an intervention in reality.

The chance of initiating an Open Learning Community depends largely on whether generative topics or key problems of considerable existential importance can be identified or not. If they are lacking, even the most committed pedagogues will first grind out their teeth on the apparent mental immobility of their potential clientele before they can create an educational movement without a true motive

Community Education/Educación Popular found new backing here and became a part of the ferment instigated by these movements. Teachers need partners, they need an alliance with other social forces to prevent their clientele from smashing vainly into hard walls which cannot be overcome. It doesn't have to be social movements, it could also be NGO's, companies, or municipalities.

Longer-term projects towards Open Learning Communities require a stable backing. This can be ministries, to the extent they themselves are capable of at least mid-term stable planning. Ministries with relatively high fluctuation rates not only on the top of the political ladder, but often in the entire staff as well, are only of limited use, as a great deal of experience has demonstrated. If one turns to NGOs one must first check whether they are built on strong foundations, and do not resemble Potemkin villages which only simulate a real existence when financial contributions appear on the horizon.

An Open Learning Community here means entering into dialog with the families living in the region, responding to their key problems (such as the acquisition of fuel and building materials or the search for additional sources of income), developing and promoting awareness of the relationships between tree-cutting and the pending ecological-economic disaster, and recruiting children as well as parents as vital supporters of a reforestation project.

In Zimbabwe there is an increasing number of orphaned children and adolescents who more or less live on the streets, since their parents have died of Aids. At the initiative of the UN Ambassador from Zimbabwe, Dr. Tichaona Jokonya, a Productive Community Highschool is to be opened about 60 kilometers outside of Harare for these abandoned children and youths, to work closely with the surrounding villages and produce products for Ethnic Interior Design out of water hyacinths growing on the nearby Lake Chivero.

The Latin-American Institute for Mental Health and Human Rights (ILAS), which is part of the Institute for the Study of Psychosocial Processes within the International Academy, has been working for many years with the victims of political repression in Chile offering social, psychotherapeutic and medical help. It has been active in research in the area of human rights and mental health, developing a model that defines trauma, illness and treatment strategies only within and in reference to the specific social, political and cultural contexts in which they occur.

ILAS has developed a network of cooperation with similar institutions in other parts of the world. Throughout the last years ILAS has been offering training and supervision to teams within Chile as well as in Peru, El Salvador, Guatemala, Nicaragua, former Yugoslavia, Germany, Switzerland, Austria and Angola. During 1996 special emphasis was put on the help to Angola and the issue of child soldiers and their demobilization. The issue of child soldiers is a difficult one.

While on the one hand there have been long-ranging international efforts to protect the rights of children and especially to limit, if not eliminate, the active participation of children in war, the use of children in armed conflict has continued, warlords seemingly not being very much impressed by international humanitarian pressure.

Furthermore some children are not officially enrolled, participate for some time and then are left behind, or accompany an elder brother, and thus do not appear in the list of child soldiers. Another problem in this context is the definition of childhood. In some countries a 12-year-old is an adult, in others a 20-year-old is an adolescent. Also it is often very difficult to distinguish between active and passive participation in war.

In short the international definition of child soldiers might fit in reference to a western industrialized society with an official army but shows serious shortcomings when we look at the crisis areas of the world. On the other hand it is useful not to forget that limited protection is better than no protection.

When we come to the issue of traumatization and reintegration into civil society once again, generalizations are difficult. War surely is traumatizing for everybody, not only for children. In many cases it is specially traumatizing for children. But in many cases we find it necessary to carefully differentiate between traumatic breakdown in terms of illness, and survival strategies in situations of turmoil and conflict. A child whose parents have been killed by one army, might very well find psychological protection in participating in the army that opposes the first one.

In many cases breakdown will only occur after war has ended, when a youth who has learned to appreciate the power of the gun suddenly has to go back to school, or tries to learn farming. In all of this the effect of violence and destruction is not less severe for the child, but the way the youth deals with these realities, be it in terms of illness, of antisocial behavior, or in terms of social integration, depends largely on the social context in which the conflict takes place.

In other words we can state that destructive, traumatic events can only be understood in reference to the specific social contexts in which they occur. Trauma and its effects can thus not be primarily defined within a medical framework, within categories like the famous Post Traumatic Stress Disorder (PTSD) but has to be understood as a long individual and social process, in which illness might or might not occur.

The concept of sequential traumatization, developed by the Dutch Psychoanalyst Hans Keilson in reference to Jewish war orphans in the Netherlands, quite adequately sums up the idea of traumatic process, proving that trauma does not stop at the end of war, but only enters into a new, decisive sequence that has to be dealt with. Using Keilson's concept and linking it to Latin American experiences with victims of state terrorism and social violence , summed up in terms like "psychosocial trauma" or "extreme traumatization" it becomes evident that the problem of child soldiers cannot be reduced to the individual, but implicates the family and the whole surrounding community.

The question is not only how ill the individual child is, but what kind of relationship can be developed between the civil population and the ex-soldier, how do they deal with their respective traumatic experiences and with the traumatized relationship existing between them. A key issue in this context is the way a society deals with its own past. This is not only a problem in terms of how much justice is being done in reference to past crimes, but how much communicational continuity can be constructed between past, present and future.

For example, experiences with child soldiers in El Salvador have shown that during war they performed quite adequately in social terms, but after the war ended, instead of reintegrating, learning, and working, they broke down, turned to drug abuse, and destroyed the economic possibilities offered them. Clearly this does not mean that war is better than peace, or that the economic or educational possibilities offered were useless. But it is obvious that the previous experience of these youths was not sufficiently taken into consideration. War is a terrorizing experience, but it also offers a dimension of adventure.

During a war the youths in question represented something, they had goals, a place in society. Now they are only dumb kids, left alone with their memories and their losses. The new future implies a loss of identity, an individual and social breakdown. In fact antisocial behavior in this context can be seen as a way to defend the former identity. Because if learning does not work, if economic development fails, then there is a strong argument in favor of returning to the existence of a soldier, bringing out the gun again.

Unfortunately international aid has not taken all these problems properly into account. Usually economic, educational and psychosocial projects are seen as three completely different areas of intervention. Trauma is seen as a health problem, lack of schooling and job training as an educational problem, and questions of productive work and survival an economic problem. While on the one hand basic necessities of survival of a given population are being satisfied, on the other side passivity is enhanced, cultural distance and non-communication seem impossible to overcome.

In Angola, for example, the United Nations are fulfilling a difficult task in helping this nation towards peace. Without the UN the war would still be going on. But it is also obvious that the discrepancies between national realities and UN-realities are huge, and continually produce misunderstandings and shortcomings. In a demobilization camp we might find barefoot soldiers handing in their weapons, walking around in the mud, and then passing through a tent in which they are registered in computers by UN personnel that maybe speak Portuguese, but definitely not the dialect the people themselves are speaking.

Many do not know the country at all, and so the registered data is not very trustworthy. When demobilization finally occurs on the basis of this data, local authorities might find that the city and the region of the home of the soldier do not match, as if an American soldier where sent to Washington D.C., California. The example might seem trivial and maybe unavoidable, but if the aim of such help really were to work towards social reintegration and the capacity to stand on one's own feet, than one would have to plan a lot more carefully how to make the people in question participate more actively in the construction of their future right from the beginning, while at the same time preparing international personnel more carefully.

The basic goal would have to be not only to stop the war but to facilitate the active construction of peace, not only to facilitate survival, but to enhance the active construction of survival strategies that persist after the international helper has gone.

It is the basic approach of this project to work towards overcoming these shortcomings of international help by the development of an Open Learning Community. In Angola, Illiteracy is close to 50%. For local authorities it is impossible to offer the formal schooling possibly necessary, simply because there are not nearly enough teachers and schools.

Many of the child solders now being demobilized have had no more than one year of schooling. Angola is a country devastated by 30 years of war, but in fact rich in natural resources. Up to now there is a group of ±8,400 registered child soldiers. In this reality it is difficult to imagine special educational activities only for them. We feel that this is not a handicap but quite to the contrary it seems to us that this offers the possibility of concentrating immediately on the communities.

Learning has to occur there; if not, in many cases it might not happen at all. The demobilization activities are also focusing on the communities in terms of material help and programs of social reintegration. In this sense Angola offers a unique opportunity to overcome the traditional splitting of projects and instead develop therapy, education, and entrepreneurship as part of community work, in terms of facilitating an Open Learning Community. The problems existing are also huge. Many areas of the country are not accessible. The general fear of a new outbreak of war is high. Horrible crimes have been committed by all the involved parties.

Children were raped and dragged from their homes, families divided, scenes of abominable violence became part of everyday life. In the communities now the situation is difficult. Officially, demobilized child soldiers receive money and survival kits that put them in an economically privileged position compared to the other villagers. Children who managed to run away from their respective army are not officially recognized, receive no help, and justly fear reprisals.

Many soldiers, adults and children had to attack their own villages. Working the land is difficult, because of a very realistic fear of the hidden land mines. In fact in Angola there more mines distributed than used in any other war before. Passivity, hopelessness, and depression are omnipresent. Bantu culture, which is the basic historic culture of Angola, implies a very special relationship to death and important debts to the dead. Death in general is considered a lack of equilibrium that has to be leveled out by the living.

Even more so, since in war the deaths were caused by crimes. If the persons who caused death do not pay their proper debt, a whole village might be punished by the vengeful dead. In this sense the returning soldiers and child soldiers carry death with them, and hence imply a very real threat to the communities. If the community cannot find a way of pacifying the dead, then the ex soldiers might be relegated from the community, or even in the worst case killed.

Therapy for a whole people is impossible, but the recognition of trauma and fear and the facilitation of grief processes is necessary. Educational or economic activities that ignore this factor are bound to fail. On the other hand grief processes without food are impossible. Only the combination of economic, educational and psychological activities have a real chance of showing positive results.

Some of these people have professional training, others don't. But the main problem is that they themselves are also highly traumatized. They have undergone the same experiences as everybody else. This condition makes them on one side more apt to do the required work, on the other hand it makes them more prone to repeat retraumatizing behavior, and apply the typical defenses of denial, splitting and authoritarian cover-ups.

This risk is even higher when such people are forced to work within formal educational or therapeutic settings, when international organizations, or magic belief in western sciences, oblige them to fill out multiple choice questionnaires with which they are supposed to diagnose the psychic alterations of the children, or when they have to speak or teach about trauma, as if it were any other subject matter, like mathematics.

Supervision and group work in terms of an open helping space in this sense are not luxuries belonging to a sophisticated psychoanalytical setting, but a basic structural need when working in this kind of context.

Mutual Learning Process

The basic methodology is linked to the situational approach combined with the theory of traumatic processes. Within the framework of Open Learning Communities, facilitators will work with local teams working in the community. Emphasis will be put on the identification of key situations, group process, and the development of alternatives in dealing with these situations.

The basic approach here will be that of a snowballing multiplier system. We will open up an office in Angola, with two permanent staff members, that will serve as permanent liaison to the local teams. This is necessary because the political situation in Angola is quite unstable and the issue in itself so sensitive, the justified national mistrust against foreign institutions so high, that continuous contact and communication on the local level is necessary.

The project will offer supervision and training to one central team, that of CCF in Angola. This team, composed of 10 persons, has up to now, 7 more teams in different regions of the country, working in the communities accompanied and supervised by them. These teams are constituted of 3 to 4 persons that again basically do multiplication work in the communities.

Three times a year ILAS will carry out 10-day workshops, using 4 days each time for working with the central team, 4 days to accompany work with the community teams and two days for public seminars, i.e. work with government and other institutions active in the same field in Angola. Two persons from the ILAS team will always attend these seminars. In order to assure continuity a basic team of 4 persons will hold the seminars, making sure that at least one person is identical from one trip to the next. The selection of the CCF team was made because up to now it is the institution working on the issue of psychosocial reintegration of child soldiers.

In the course of the project, the central target group might become bigger, basically through the association of new institutions and government agencies working on the same task. Close contact will be held to MINARS, the ministry of social assistance, that has to carry out the central rehabilitation programs. Most probably supervision will be extended to their teams, carried out as much as possible by the groups that have received training from us. If in the course of the project it is possible to develop the perspective of a nation wide campaign, we will support the effort. But we certainly prefer to start small, show that the concept works, and accompany the national initiatives to the issue instead of intervening from above, from outside, without a real basis in the country.

Documentation is a central task of the project not only in reference to its own work, but also in reference to other projects around the world. The basic idea is to construct an archive with a corresponding thesaurus that can serve as reference for any interested institution. Apart from the collection of published articles one important problem is that many people do interesting work but never write about it, and if they do, feel obliged to explain their activities in traditional western-oriented scientific language, thereby often falsifying and hiding what they really do.

Documentation of our own work will basically consist of careful protocols of everything we do: taped recordings, written articles, critical evaluation of our project partners on a regular basis, as well as a film documentation of the development of the project. The problem with film documentations about wars and their aftermath is that they usually cannot show an individual and collective process.

Afterwards throughout the three years this will be periodically repeated, but only in the last year of the project will a complete film finally be edited, discussed with the participants, and actually produced. The cost of such a production is comparatively high, and we do not propose to finance it completely from within the project. But we do wish to have enough basic financing for this activity so that matching funds can be found. Another important point is that we plan to produce manuals and a book about the project.

The manuals will refer to local specific issues of the project that can be used in other areas of the country. Internationally they will refer to our basic approach, to the techniques we used, what was helpful and what not, to the kind of framework that is necessary when confronting similar situations in other parts of the world. The objective here is to produce manuals that can be read and used by professionals as well as lay persons. In the book we intend to sum up as well as theoretically reflect the development of the project.

Networking is a highly difficult task always, and especially so when working in the area of trauma. Usually people are so immersed in their own traumatic reality, that although theoretically they all find networking a good idea, they never seem to find the time for it. We furthermore hope to develop a communicative structure that will permit participating institutions to mutually evaluate their work, thereby making it better and more apt to achieve the eternal search for funding.

In the long run participants will thus obtain a mark of quality, comparable to the star system used by hotels. Using Internet, e-mail etc. we will start slowly, building up a trustworthy network from the beginning onwards, not because it is big - although we would not mind that - but because it is good.

The quantitative extension of public education in many countries during the 60's and 80's has undeniably brought about a certain amount of success, but at the same time led to a large-scale spreading of qualitative shortcomings, such as high dropout levels, rigid forms of teaching, the poor relation between some curricula and reality, and an examination system blown up out of all proportion. The NISBA project wants to make use of its particular profile to search for solutions to some of these problems, and point out ways to overcome them.

Intercultural education means educating for international understanding right at one's own doorstep. NISBA will be a place where children of different nations, religions, and socio-cultural origins can learn to live together in an atmosphere of tolerance and solidarity. Intercultural education means on the one hand making sense of your own culture, finding your identity in your own culture - to understand culture not as something from a museum, but a living force and source of new impulses without ripping out the old moorings. On the other hand, intercultural education includes the ability of looking beyond your own horizons to comprehend that we live in one world together, and desire to accept each other in peace and mutual freedom.

In many countries the relationship between the educational system and the employment system is badly out of balance. The European myth fed by its privileged past, that the educational system would prepare qualified workers and the employment system subsequently offer the appropriate jobs, has turned out to be just as deceptive a belief as the hope, for example, which university graduates harbor in developing countries, that they will automatically receive jobs in the administration of large companies or in the civil service.

In view of ever keener competition on the world market, education will increasingly only then mean better jobs when people learn to land on their own feet and to create jobs appropriate to world market conditions. Among other things this presupposes that professional pedagogues - hitherto used to an almost lifelong secure march through pedagogical institutions, and usually defensive by nature - also learn this lesson for themselves and act as appropriate role models. It is not enough here to limit oneself to advancing qualified employees, as if to imply that employer qualities such as innovative marketable ideas simply fall from heaven. Instead, it is necessary to promote an education for entrepreneurial behavior, an education for economy from below which begins at an early age and perceives entrepreneurial activity less as a personal peculiarity, and more as a basic qualification of the citoyen.

With this in mind, educational processes, subjects, and institutions can become counter-productive problems in themselves: the processes, as long as they adhere to a type of learning which barely accounts for the uncertainties of learning in real situations; the subject matter, as long as they ignore and suppress key problems of life under difficult conditions; the institutions, as long as they tend to represent the opposite of an entrepreneurial model in regard to structure and organization.

The entire structure and program of colonial-style schools counteract the entrepreneurial potential of the majority of the population. As it is, one could argue with de Soto that aspiring countries on the development threshold can just bear this sort of education system, because the learning opportunities of the economic environment are large enough that graduates can complete their actual apprenticeship out in the world. Aware of this chance, they don't run much of a risk of becoming "permanent youths" at some pedagogical institution.

Entrepreneurship is understood here as a fundamental force in the socially and ecologically responsible formation of the world: ethics pay. The entrepreneur NISBA will be trying to promote from childhood on is a visionary who recognizes a problem, develops an entrepreneurial idea arising from it, and tests and implements that idea on the market. NISBA will support children, adolescents, and involved adults in further developing entrepreneurial ideas.

NISBA is a resource for the generation of such ideas - the plan is to realize projects locally with local partners, hence contributing to community development. It would certainly be desirable when students who have graduated from the school take their ideas with them as spin-offs to be implemented elsewhere.

The international discussion about school curriculum and its further development refers to, among other things, the following shortcomings and weaknesses:

— The curriculum is geared too one-sidedly to academic subjects and the scientific disciplines underlying them, risking a loss of connection with reality.

— The style of repetitive study and learning material by heart is not suited to promoting the transfer of knowledge or encouraging the skill of applying what has been learned to complex real situations.

— A networked, interdisciplinary mode of thought is hampered by the fixation on subjects with their own inherent logic. The segmentation of learning material into small units hinders the ability of recognizing interconnections and relationships. The sheer amount of subject matter makes concentration on fundamentals even harder.

— The development of the school curriculum takes too little account of social developments and requirements; time is not taken to make well-researched situation analyses, and too few studies examine the kinds of situations in which graduates must later be qualified to work.

Learning is oriented towards real-life situations. "Learning through life" means that learning processes should be encouraged in such real-life situations as much as possible. In this case, learning takes place not so much within parameters of a didactically arranged pretense of security (where problem presentation, solution route, and solution itself are already known beforehand), but rather in the openness of complex reality.

It is an experience-oriented, inquisitive, experimenting, discovering type of learning in which theory and practice, reflection and action are all intimately interconnected with each other. Children have a right to learn material in context, to relate social with factual learning, and not be helplessly subjected to merely reduced and tailored forms of knowledge, but rather be encouraged to understand and explain the social contexts of meaningful activity. Children have a right to take part in designing situations in which they learn and act. They want to be challenged in their strengths, and not spoon-fed with pedagogical tranquilizers of occupational therapy.

They have a right to be children and regarded as such (but not subjected to infantile treatment). Those who desire to help children on their way should do so with awareness of their individual development and chances of growth. To be empowered in real-life situations does not only mean possessing the necessary survival techniques, but also includes enhancing personal strength and the ability to entertain radical or different thoughts; it can also even mean the unhindered development of a craze or passion, the encouragement of wild play, or deep involvement in the arts, or expressions of feelings and bodily senses, movement and consciousness.

The context of normative behavior is to be explained over and over again, to counteract the split between 'moral' and 'technically instrumental competence' Educators and teachers do not behave as if giving orders from the command post, but rather as partners and impulse-givers: asking, curious, sensitive, also learning. An open, situation-dependent planning replaces the usual rigid ritual.

As with their children, the parents also take on a more central role in what is happening. To the extent that they can be present and want to be involved, they act as participants and active experts. Parents can offer a great variety of competent skills in key situations.

They help build bridges to the community. The situation approach reacts sensitively to minorities, opposes segregation, favors the integration of handicapped persons, invites interaction with other strangers, and values cultural variety in one world. The situation approach is always a form of community education, aims to open up pedagogical institutions and remove walls that block our view. It counteracts the exclusion of childhood and youth from real-life activity, interprets learning as an integral part of community development, depends on the cooperation of professional pedagogues and competent members of the entire community, and taps learning venues within the community.

With the situation approach and the structural concept of the curriculum, a decisive step is attempted to make reality (to the extent it contains facts relevant to the issue) the immediate reference point for the development of educational processes and subject matter.

This approach draws on sources of knowledge - academic as well as experience-based - and focuses them on real-life situations with their concomitant problem areas. The curriculum is hence organized according to key topics, problems, and situations and not according to subjects or departments. It does not follow the structure of any academic discipline, but rather instrumentalizes relevant methods and subject matters in order to explain and manage the situation.

Individualized Teaching

Some schools can be heard from far off: the teacher loudly speaks phrases, the whole class answers as one. Old-fashioned schools of this kind are to a large degree products of the colonial era, their classroom teaching methods still reflecting the spirit of the 19th and early 20th centuries. Teachers concentrate on covering each small portion of the fixed curriculum, and try not only to tame the horde of young lions in the class, but also bring them all to do the same thing at the same time.

The style of mechanical learning employed is the most unsuitable conceivable for making sense of interrelationships, retaining what one has learned (even after the next exam), and applying knowledge gained. This is where a disastrous vicious circle of dequalification must be broken: insufficiently trained teachers behave like slaves to a detailed prescribed curriculum and force their students to reduce the great diversity of learning and experience down to the learning of textbooks by heart.

When this mechanical system, which clearly contradicts the fundamental discoveries of modern learning theories, is then further underpinned by frequent tests and exams, one could even maintain that such a school is in the position of actually mutilating the qualifying potential of the next generation.

Good test results achieved within this mechanism reveal very little about the ability to retain what one has learned, or creatively apply it in any given real situation. Frontal class teaching will be a seldom occurrence in NISBA. Instead, relying on the knowledge gained in modern learning theory, a researching, discovering, active kind of learning is favored.

Learning will take place individually or in small teams, and the biography and learning background of every child will be taken into account. In contrast to repetitive learning which takes place within parameters of false security (where problem presentation, solution route, and solution itself are always already known beforehand), here the learning processes are of a much more open nature.

Naturally there will still be some 'right' and 'wrong' answers. But in real-life situations there are often a number of different options which have to be compared and considered before making a decision. In any case, learning in connection with entrepreneurship also means learning how to think strategically while dealing with uncertainties, practicing to take calculated risks.

There is a veritable arsenal of teaching methods and forms of pedagogical organization that serve these goals: teaching in small groups, learning and acting in projects, open or informal education, orienting the time frame to the task at hand and the current project (and not the other way around), team teaching, mixed-aged groups and cross-generational learning (where it makes sense to do so). Classrooms can be transformed into learning workshops.

At the same time, the limits of traditional school spaces will be dissolved: all the students will work with laptops and personal computers, and be able to communicate directly with teachers and other students electronically. Everyone will have access to libraries all over the world.

In this interactive learning development, the concept of "classroom" will surpass the traditional classroom. In developing their projects, students will also be able to make use of multimedia designs, computer assisted drafting, the information highway, and graphic and desktop publishing tools. In this regard it is important to correctly evaluate the instrumental role played by electronic media: Such tools are an enormous help but not an end in themselves. Real experience is always more important than virtual reality

NISBA assumes a consensus concerning basic values of a democratically organized community. Children and young people can claim the right to handle situations with increasing autonomy and competence; at the same time they are challenged to show solidarity with others or act with ecological responsibility. NISBA can be considered as a polis in the sense borrowed from ancient Greece: a small-scale model of a democratic state. The pupils increasingly take over functions and responsibilities and share these with the adults.

Life in the Open Learning Community offers many chances of bringing a strong sense of self and an equally strong sense of community into a healthy relationship with each other, and preparing decisions by means of a democratic process of consensus building. Democracy does not exclude leadership - on the contrary, democracy depends on good leadership. Business enterprises also need strong leadership and the loyalty of their employees, but it is to the advantage of any business to keep up a meaningful dialog with its teams.

The pupils will live separately according to sex, but not according to nationality or cultural heritage. Tolerance and respect is thus a highly valued virtue. Social responsibility is practiced, for instance, by work in some social or technical service such as a rescue service, the school fire department, technical relief organization, social services or environmental conservation service.

The topography of the Open Learning Community contains a local network of facilities in Bali, and extends further into the wide world (for example of the High Seas High School). The NISBA kindergarten will be neither a daycare facility nor a preschool, but will rather emphasize and promote the creativity, curiosity, and motivation of the children. It will allow the children to be children without babying them. It will promote and encourage them, not through mechanical drills, but by helping them in their own discoveries of their inner and outer worlds.

The kindergarten accepts children of Balinese or Indonesian origin as well as children from the international community living on Bali. The following characteristics of its pedagogical concept are the most important:

— *Learning in real-life situations*: Children learn how to cope with situations here and now, not some hypothetical situation in the distant future, not adult situations. And coping does not only mean surviving in situations, but also being able to grasp them as alterable and oneself as effective.

— *The connection between social and factual learning*: this works against alienated learning. Away from separating initial mathematical operations from social contexts, away from promoting a kind of speech that has nothing to do with own experience, away from learning that is devoid of sense. The primacy of social learning applies.

Factual learning is important, but is to be integrated into the process of social learning and whenever possible with reference to social contexts. The children acquire knowledge, skills, and abilities necessary to understand and create real-life situations. Atomized, tailored learning which does not lead to comprehensible meaningful connections is avoided.

Children take part in creating situations in which they are involved, and in the life within and outside the kindergarten. They cooperate in selecting and planning activities; not everything is simply arranged for them by the kindergarten teacher. They are encouraged to influence situations and change them. Self initiative and responsibility are promoted. The children experience the sense of norms in real-life situations. They do not receive lectures on norms, but are given the opportunity of making sense of them in context, and to negotiate their activity in them correspondingly.

The kindergarten teachers secure a promotion of basic qualifications appropriate to the stage of development, taking into account the individual characteristics of each child and their different levels of development.

The kindergarten teachers promote the diversity of the children's' expressive possibilities. They encourage activity involving all the senses, diverse forms of movement alternating with quiet and thoughtfulness, free play as well as creative and artistic activity, the expression of feelings and emotional intelligence Children have a right to increasingly understand the world, themselves, and their social environment.

They gradually become acquainted with their own culture and learn to respect the cultures of others, step by step they become more familiar with the world of the spirit, tradition, and religion. The children live and learn in mixed age groups as much as possible. Three-year-olds often accept more from five-year-olds than from adults, and older children can develop real empathy for the needs of younger children. Outside in real life, everything is learned among people of mixed ages. On the other hand the mixing of age groups is no dogma - there can also be situations in which peer groups want to be among themselves.

Learning for life situations also means learning in life situations. Hence fields of activity outside of the kindergarten will be integrated, so that the kindergarten truly becomes a part of the social network. The kindergarten teacher remains in close dialog with parents and families. The parents are not just onlookers, but rather personal authorities on the situations of their children. They take part in the kindergarten whenever they want to. In order to do this, it is important that the kindergarten be flexible with parents with regard to time and organization.

Pupils of other nationalities need an international school. In order to make both alternatives a possible reality, a solution which allows for both kinds of schools is necessary. Each school has to fulfill its own requirements, but the two schools are more than that: they are to work closely together The school levels of the Indonesian School are divided into a Primary School for grades 1-6, a Junior High School for grades 7-9, and a Senior High School for grades 10-12.

Graduation is documented with the granting of an Indonesian Ijazah certificate. The school levels of the International School consist of a 4-year Primary School, a Secondary School for grades 5-10, and an International College for grades 11 and 12, which is completed with an International Baccalaureat.

The boundaries between the school grades will not have very much particular importance in daily practice, but rather only represent a general demarcation. Actually the main thing is that pupils in grades 5-12 grow up together and are encouraged and challenged according to their general age level.

As of the fifth school year, children can be accepted to the Boarding School. This applies to Indonesian children as well as those of other nationalities. Most likely a small portion of these boarding school students will attend the national school; the majority will attend the international school. The national school could participate in the special NISBA profile in agreement with the Indonesian Minister of Education and the competent authorities, hence acting as a model for other such schools.

The national primary school adheres to the Indonesian curriculum. Next to Indonesian, English functions as the second teaching language. The goal is to achieve proficient bilingual fluency. English is the teaching language in the international primary school. Other mother tongues will be encouraged as much as possible.

The curriculum is oriented on the International Baccalaureat Primary Years (IBPYP), whereby local relationships play a considerable role. In both schools it is important that the pedagogical principles are continued as they were practiced in the kindergarten (from which at least some of the children will have transferred), and adjusted for older ages. There should be no cultural break between the preschool and school areas. Getting rid of frontal class teaching involves more than re-arranging the classroom furniture in a more casual manner, especially as long as the teacher continues to determine classroom activity to the smallest detail.

Nevertheless, an open class begins with redesigning the classrooms. They will be set up into experience zones, almost labyrinths, so that different activities can be carried out at the same time: for instance math, reading and writing, or art. Learning takes place individually or in small groups, often crossing disciplines. Open teaching does not mean an unprepared lesson. The teachers are well aware of the individual learning history of each child, and relate directly to where that child is.

The curriculum contains a foundation of knowledge which the children all know they are to acquire. But the children can, in agreement with their teachers, organize when and what they do in the week. They decide when to read, or do an experiment on magnetism, or whatever. Furthermore there are other projects and freely chosen activities. The day often begins with a gathering of such a group in a large circle: the children and teacher consult with each other, make plans, exchange ideas and suggestions. There is a strong atmosphere of self-discipline, and learning is sparked by the joy of discovery and open curiosity.

The children supervise their weekly plan themselves - they check off what they have already completed and look ahead at all they wanted to accomplish. At the end of the school day everyone meets once again in the large circle to share experiences and prepare for the next day. The teachers offer stimulation and ideas, provide necessary materials, help in solving problems, show how and where research can be carried out on a question. They keep diary accounts of the experiences and activities of their children in order to recognize progress made and point out where particular stimulation or support is needed. An open classroom has more chance of success when two teachers work together.

As the national primary school, the national secondary school (consisting of Junior and Senior High School) adheres to the Indonesian curriculum, with English complementing Indonesian as second teaching language. The international secondary school operates on the same principle as the primary school: English as teaching language, and promotion of other mother tongues whenever possible.

Education is not conceivable without 'enlightenment'. It does not deserve to be called education if it is not able to help the individual to use his own mind without being imposed upon and controlled by another. Education is the path used by children and adolescents to find their way in this world, to define themselves and discover that they are able to change things, that they have responsibilities, that they can be aware. Certainly one cannot understand anything without knowing something, but one can know much without understanding. Knowledge which does not serve greater understanding remains unfruitful and can even become extremely dangerous.

Today we would speak of 'holistic' and 'learning by experience', perhaps also of learning by doing. - Schools are not only there to instruct the heads, but just as much to educate and develop the senses, feelings, physical health, manual dexterity. The senses, feelings, body and hands also have to be able to have experiences which encourage and promote them and thus help 'educate' the person as a human being."

Tourism is frequently staged far away from the truly interesting situations and opportunities of the country. Tourism can contribute to the destruction of regional cultures. However, that properly handled tourism can support and promote regional cultures and contribute to their development, that an individualized, authentic tourism can act as culturally enriching and serve ethnic understanding, that it can provide great pleasure as well as be the economically better concept to make intelligent friends and partners out of the previous opposing "dumb tourist" and broad mass of "natives".

On the one hand the Center is a program which brings guests together with culturally, politically, and economically leading families of the local and regional area in Bali, and allows them topersonally enjoy their hospitality. On the other hand it provides guests who are looking for social and cultural contrasts with expeditions and projects concerning various island realities. All the projects have a playful and enjoyable character. The 'scholarly concept' of the Center is founded on elements of action research, discovery learning, and sensual experience. It does not assume expert knowledge, but only a healthy common sense, curiosity, and the joy of discovery.

The research carried out by the guests makes sense, and is not intended as occupational therapy, and most of the projects are result-oriented for both the guests and the island. No guest must have the feeling of only standing around in the role of the goose who lays the golden eggs. The projects are variable in length. They can be long-term (in which case individual guests participate for a while, then leave) or as short-term as a single day. These projects are dramatically designed according to a varied scheme, with climax, action, and relaxation phases.

One of its essential aspects is that native people and guests get to know each other, and that guests make contacts among each other as well. The guests can document the results of these activities themselves if they so desire. A guest library will be set up. so that the progress of the various projects can be followed and reconstructed for new guests who join in later, or for those guests who might return and who want to check up on what has been done in their absence. The activities will be reported on locally and internationally: on the local level, the native people experience the results of the projects.

The students act as trace-seekers, the developer of paths into an interesting reality. They take care of the guests during their research activities and learn by direct participation. In doing so they also learn how to work with the guests in an articulate, culturally competent and imaginative manner. The curriculum of this Center deals with general knowledge concerning tourism and management, as well as specific historical, religious, cultural, artistic, architectural, geographical, biological, and ecological knowledge of Bali. A cultural authentic tourism as practiced here in a small-scale model also makes good sense.

In US, the majority of the pupils will originate from places far away from Bali. For their parents this means that visiting their children involves a great deal of travel. In order to make their stay on the island as pleasant as possible, on the one hand parents are invited to participate in activities of the school when and as they please, and on the other hand they are to be made to feel as comfortable as possible as guests.

3

Ethical Issues of Technology in Education

The indicator systems are top-down, published, management systems, addressing primarily the issue of public accountability. The systems are also being used by groups in New Zealand, Australia and Hong Kong, and with international schools in 30 countries. These systems would not have grown had they not been cost-effective for schools. This demanded the technical excellence that makes possible the provision of one hundred percent accurate data in a very timely fashion.

An infrastructure of powerful hardware and ever-improving software is needed, along with extensive programming to provide carefully chosen graphical and tabular presentations of data, giving at-a-glance comparative information. Highly skilled staff, always learning new techniques, have been essential, especially as we move into computer-based data collection. It has been important to adopt transparent, readily understood methods of data analysis where we are satisfied that these are accurate, and to model the processes that produce the data.

Ethical issues are surprisingly often lurking in technical decisions. For example, reporting outcomes from a continuous measure in terms of the percent of students who surpassed a certain level, produces unethical behavior: a concentration of teaching on borderline students. Distortion of behavior and data corruption are ever-present concerns in indicator systems. The systems we describe would have probably failed to thrive had they not addressed schools' on-going concerns about education.

Moreover, data interpretation can only be completed in the schools, by those who know all the factors involved. Thus the commitment to working closely and collaboratively with schools in "distributed research" is important, along with "measuring what matters"... not only achievement. In particular the too-facile interpretation of correlation as causation that characterized much school effectiveness research had to be avoided and the need for experimentation promoted and demonstrated.

Over the last 15 years, indicator systems that have developed, and attracted support and subscriptions from about a third of the schools in England where we work on a scale many times greater than any other group. And also developed a linked Curriculum, Evaluation and Management Centre at the University of Canterbury in Christchurch, New Zealand, and have the pleasure of welcoming participation from scattered schools in thirty countries.

The development of the indicator systems in the CEM Centre is unusual if not unique in that schools themselves have chosen to participate. The systems are therefore professional, ground-up, developments, that stand in contrast to "top-down" indicator systems created, and sometimes imposed, by state and local authorities. The interests of both kinds of systems should ultimately, however, be coincident: to improve education. An indicator can be defined as an item of information collected at regular intervals to track the performance of a system.

The indicator systems that have formed the basis of our learning are all designed to feed back valuable information of interest to teachers and administrators in schools and colleges. The indicator or information systems as significantly empowering schools as they participate with a university in 'distributed research'. The issue of public accountability must also addressed by indicator systems. The design of each system has been driven by the need to measure outcomes that matter along with relevant covariates so that fair comparisons can be made. Process variables are measured in some of the systems, but only to generate hypotheses, not to make judgements.

In 1997, Fitz-Gibbon can be found on the website for the Qualifications and Curriculum Authority. The studies carried out contributed to ongoing debates of both a technical and ethical nature.

Technical issues include those procedural problems that must be solved if an indicator system is to be of high quality and run in a timely, efficient and effective fashion. Indicators need to be based on adequate samples, have appropriate levels of reliability, good validity, and above all, positive reactivity. These are technical terms straight out of research methods courses, but they go to the heart of indicator systems, and any practical use of data. The data must be of research quality, otherwise it will confuse rather than guide.

In 1983, technical sophistication was no more than batch-processing using a mainframe. The mainframe could deliver capital letters and stars and eventually an adequate type-face could be constructed via embedded commands in a special program that could produce quite nicely spaced upper and lower case printing. Access to a data entry service was essential and it was quickly obvious, as the volume of data increased, that adequate data verification techniques had to be built-in.

At first, this was by double-entry, which was not satisfactory; followed by data checking on entry, which required some programming to prevent out-of-range data being entered and to ensure the data went into the right columns on the 80-column cards. From these humble and clumsy beginnings, today to a situation where extensive programming is used, optical mark recognition assists some data entry, computer based tests that can record responses directly and be delivered across intranets and internets are becoming essential features of indicator systems.

Not only is data translated into meaningful sentences contingent upon the data-values, but also into graphs that, for example, change colour when differences are statistically significant. Without this level of technical expertise, data will not be attractive and easy to access by busy teachers, the turn-around of data will be slow and errors will creep in. Schools want data quickly, within weeks of examination results becoming available. And they want the data 100 per cent accurate.

In most research projects, if a small percentage of the data doesn't match, this can simply be reported and ignored, but in indicator systems, schools want every single student accounted for. In consequence, not only must there be teams of expert programmers, but also very high capacity computing equipment. Facilities for printing CDs are helpful, as special, user-friendly software is developed to assist schools in their own explorations of their data.

CDs can also be used to deliver computerised tests. The data files returned to schools also need to interface easily with schools' management information software such as timetabling and staff deployment. If the technical infrastructure is effective, data turn-around quick, data presentation attractive and readily interpreted, then the indicator systems will probably grow and this growth itself demands further technical capabilities, such as running a high-capacity server and creating a central database that can be accessed by researchers and secretaries alike.

This central database needs to be relational in order to store efficiently the hundreds of thousands of students with hundreds of variables attached to each student in thousands of schools over many years. It must have an extremely friendly front end, so that secretaries can readily track the mail-out of questionnaires and the return of data, plus a massive invoicing system if individual schools can join the project and pay on their own account. Finally the infrastructure needs communication on a regular basis with all schools. Newsletters, a website and conferences are important, particularly as teachers become conference presenters and have a credibility with fellow teachers that researchers lose after some years away from the classroom.

If the infrastructure for indicator systems can be created, then a cost-effective system is feasible. It consider the design of such a system, including choosing what to measure, collecting the data, analysing, reporting and interpreting the data.

A few indicators cannot reflect the complexity of institutions and will undermine the system as gaming takes hold. Given a few indicators, the effort is focused on these concerns alone. Furthermore it is difficult to know which indicators will become important in the future, so that what is now considered to be a key indicator may become of less concern in the future. Multiple indicators for complex organisations are a fairer representation of the multiple realities within each than is any attempt to assign a single label, whether this label be numerical (e.g. average value added) or verbal (e.g. 'coasting', 'failing').

Bloom's Taxonomy of Educational Objectives identified affective, cognitive and psychomotor outcomes that can be taken to include behavioural outcomes. The distinction between aptitudes and achievements is an important distinction in the cognitive area. Clearly money matters, so economic indicators are important.

The essence of schooling is who is taught what for how long and by what methods and these concerns can, following the OECD practice be called 'Flow'. Eventually all of these aspects should have indicators. The indicators could be collected from various groups such as students, teachers, heads, school districts, states, or parents, the community, the voters.

Most indicators could be an input, an output or a long-term outcome and may also be related to a process. Thus a comprehensive classification of indicators can be developed and this also will require a relational database if the measures are to be efficiently stored.

Prior achievement is an excellent predictor of subsequent achievement, but each student's level of prior achievement will be partly influenced by the effectiveness of the previous stage of schooling. One teacher's output is then another teacher's input. Teachers quite reasonably worry that if they promote high achievement at one age it may be more difficult to show high rates of progress (value added) subsequently.

The introduction of baseline tests as an alternative to achievement input measures has provided an important alternative approach. The purpose of our baseline tests is not to stamp labels on students, but to predict how easy or difficult it will be to get students through the next set of examinations. What is needed for these tests, then, is typical performance, not maximum performance.

In the secondary school use tape recordings for test administration so that all schools present students with the same information in the same tone of voice using exactly the same words and the same timing of each of the subtests. Old IQ tests, in contrast, are often administered in ways that are not properly standardised from school to school. The baseline tests to obtain good predictions of subsequent achievement. The aim has been to obtain quick and efficient measures by using item formats and tasks that require many responses from the pupil that are instantly recorded and therefore add up very quickly to a good predictor of general academic performance.

These tests are in some cases remarkably efficient. For example, in 20 minutes the PIPS individually administered adaptive baseline assessment for 4 and 5 year olds obtains measures that predict subsequent progress in mathematics and reading with correlations of about 0.7. At the secondary school level, our baseline test (the MidYIS test, part of the Middle Years Information System takes 45 minutes of working time and predicts subsequent achievement with correlations of about 0.7, depending upon the subject such as English or mathematics. The MidYIS test was chosen by the prestigious independent schools for a compulsory baseline.

In addition to prior achievement or baseline measures, are there other important covariates? The best source of information about relevant covariates is not what people write about, but what the data shows. Much is written, for example, of the impact of socio-economic status on achievement, but at the pupil level the correlation is generally about 0.3, thus implying that about 9 per cent of variance in the outcomes will be accounted for by knowing the socio-economic status of the student.

In contrast, cognitive measures predict about 50 per cent of subsequent variation. To obtain adequate prediction of subsequent achievement ... and therefore the fairest data for teachers...there is no adequate alternative to a cognitive test. In addition to the cognitive indicators we need to address the affective and social domains. In Victoria, Australia, there is extensive use of questionnaires to students, to staff in schools and to parents.

Currently, in the Curriculum, Evaluation and Management Centre, concentrate on questionnaires to students, since education is primarily aimed at the students who are compulsory under the treatment indicator systems. Students can tell questionnaires how much they like school, how much they like an individual subject, whether they feel safe in school, their aspirations for the future, their relationships with teachers, their health, traumas in their lives, how they are taught, and how interesting they find each subject, etc., etc.

For children in their first year at school also ask teachers to rate the children's attention, impulsivity and activity levels. Certainly, when schools first join an indicator system, they can feel quite overwhelmed by the amount of data that is returned from a fully developed system. For schools in the first few years of participation 'Keep it simple, stupid' might be a good motto, especially as there is evidence that giving people too much data is de-motivating.

Another wide variety of systems of indicators that involve paper- or computer-based tests, as well as 'basic' or 'extended' versions, the latter including hundreds of variables. The system that will involve on-line administration of data collection and permit matrix sampling and the inclusion of choice, by students or other respondents to questionnaires, of the domains in which they would like to express their views and opinions.

This will need close attention to the reliability of the data collected. Thus the matrix sampling will use scales as the unit of sampling rather than items. Having decided on how to measure the outcomes that matter, one is not finished with the creation of indicators. Just as prior achievement predicts subsequent achievement, so prior attitudes will predict subsequent attitudes, and in order to compare like with like need to use regression analyses and look at the residuals.

The prediction appears not to be so strong as in the cognitive area, perhaps due to less reliable measures, but about 25 percent of the variance of final attitudes in secondary schools is usually predictable from knowing intake attitudes. An indicator system consisting of dependent variables with appropriate covariates is a complete indicator system.

However, an indicator system is only a step along the way to trying to understand what works, and how schooling can be improved. Consequently, some of the indicator systems include process variables such as descriptions of methods of teaching and learning for which students in the 16-18 age range report the frequency of use. Process indicators serve to generate hypotheses and most importantly, they stimulate discussion of teaching methods among staff in schools and as such are valuable.

As Berliner argued, qualitative data are powerful. Early in the ALIS project, one school was constantly at the bottom of the set of participating schools on a scale assessing attitude to school. It paid very little attention to this fact but then open-ended questions were introduced into the data collection and students' comments were typed up and made available to the schools. The typing disguised students' handwriting and kept the feedback anonymous.

When the school read statements like 'We are treated like fifth formers without uniform', 'Staff are sarcastic', 'I wish I'd gone to another school' this qualitative data had an impact that was immediate and led to a re-design of the provision for subsequent students. Having had that experience, the school then watched the quantitative attitude indicators with more concern and continue to provide typed-up responses to open-ended questions.

The cognitive data collection is standardised so that the same procedures are followed in every school. This standardisation of data collection is important in collecting data that can be validly compared from school to school. A particular threat to the validity of attitude data could arise from demand characteristics.

If students are being asked if they like the school and whether they get on well with teachers yet teachers are looking over students' shoulders, or if the students feel that their questionnaires will be scrutinised by teachers, then the situation becomes subject to possible pressures and influences that could inhibit honest responding.

In the secondary school projects, the tape recording that administers the cognitive test introduces the questionnaire part of the data collection by noting that if there is anything they don't understand they should not raise their hand and ask questions because the teacher cannot come to their desk to help them, since the teacher will be staying at the front of the class in order to avoid seeing the responses on any of the questionnaires. Of course this procedure requires that students can read the questionnaires and this may not always be the case.

The creation of a monitoring system involves a great many decisions and, as a system grows and there is feedback from the users of the system, there is a need to be responsive and flexible whilst holding firm to fundamental principles.

In developing an on-entry assessment for 4-5 year olds the intention was that the data would be kept until the children reached the first statutory assessment three years later. But many reception class teachers suggested that we should assess the students again at the end of their first year at school using an extended version of the on-entry assessment.

The outcome measures should, of course, be curriculum-embedded, high-stakes, authentic tests that reflect work actually taught and worth teaching in the classroom. The use of a standardised multiple choice measure of reading comprehension, for example, is not likely to be fair to schools since teachers may not be able to influence reading comprehension skills once students can read.

In other words, there is a problem of lack of sensitivity to instruction. The matching of data from different sources can only be efficiently done by the use of unique identifiers. These preferably should be identifiers containing check digits and the computing facilities to make sure that no identifier is mis-entered.

Einstein said that everything should be as simple as possible, but no simpler. This is a wise, but very challenging, piece of advice. One cannot know how simple a data analysis can be until one has done both simple and complicated analyses and compared the results with representative sets of real data so that one is looking not only at theoretical models but also at actual magnitudes.

The same data sets using ordinary least squares and multilevel models, and found, as we had found previously, that the average residuals indicating the so-called 'value added' scores for departments or schools, correlated at worst 0.93, and more usually higher, up to 0.99 on the two analyses. Thus it was possible to have the data valid and 'readily understood' by using simple regression. The multi-level analysis, requiring special software and a postgraduate course in statistical analysis, was in contrast to the ordinary least squares analysis that could be taught in primary schools.

In UK, the ordinary least squares analysis can certainly be presented to schools so that most members of staff understand the analysis and can use software to re-analyse data as necessary. This accessibility of the data along with the atmosphere of joint investigation (distributed research) probably helped to encourage acceptance of the indicator systems, unlike the situation that sadly seems to have arisen in Tennessee where a highly ambitious, yearly multi-level analysis was tracking students and teachers.

The development of multilevel modelling or hierarchical linear models is admirable, provides efficient calculations and rather different error terms, but to use these procedures in day to day indicator system work is likely to lead to less acceptance of the analysis by teachers.

Moreover, it is somewhat akin to applying a correction for relativity when considering the momentum of a moving train: theoretically correct, but in scientific terms, an ill-advised tendency to over-precision. A recommendation in the Value Added National Project was that prompt initial feedback should be based on very simple value added measures taking account of prior achievement and using ordinary least squares regression methods that any school could adopt and replicate.

Professor Robin Plackett, winner of two gold medals from the Royal Statistical Society, emphasised in his lectures, usually in his opening sentences that the question to ask, first and foremost, was what processes produced the data. The essence of good statistical modelling is to model the process that produces the data.

From the very start, with the A Level Information System in 1982-83, it was clear that the regression line for mathematics was quite different from the regression line for English and implied that for the same level of prior achievement students would come out with two grades lower taking the Advanced examination in mathematics than they would taking Advanced English. Regrettably, other researchers have simply taken the results of all examinations and assumed that the scales could be combined without any adjustment.

Having thus confused the data, sophisticated multilevel models were applied to find that there were differential slopes, i.e. slopes that differed for high and low ability intakes. It was even suggested that teachers may be to blame for concentrating on some groups more than others. This was poor data interpretation since a confound (different subjects with different regression lines) was being attributed to teachers' actions without any corroborating evidence.

The presentation of data needs to change according to the experience of the school. A school just beginning to get feedback data needs a few clear diagrams and a telephone helpline in case of questions. Schools that have become used to receiving data and have, despite some initial rejection from some departments found it to be useful and credible, start to make more and more use of the data.

It therefore becomes valuable to them to have the data provided in Excel spreadsheets, possibly with pre-programmed macros, or in specially prepared software that allows them to undertake procedures such as separating out teaching groups, aggregating by curriculum area, dropping students who have missed substantial amounts of schooling, and adding students for whom data was missing. Increasingly, as we move from paper-based feedback to sending disks we provide instant feedback. Eventually, with tight encryption techniques this will be directly over the internet.

It has been important, for example, that baseline tests are not seen as predicting exact outcomes. Fifty per cent of the variation in outcomes is predictable but that means that 50 per cent is not. This problem was confronted very early in that schools were in some cases preventing students from taking advanced mathematics had they not received a C grade or higher in earlier mathematics courses. When data from a large number of schools was available, in some of which students had been allowed to take the advanced course even having not done well earlier, it was possible to present what we now call 'Chances graphs'.

This empirical distribution has great credibility with teachers and students. It is data that actually happened and if it happened once it can happen again. Thus, the low-achieving student is encouraged to recognise that many low achieving students from the previous year well exceeded the average predicted grade for that starting point. By representing their 'chances', we remove the opposition rightly felt to labelling students with single predicted grades and provide actual data that is motivating for students.

Compliance with freedom of information legislation and other relevant laws may require that considerable amounts of data are published. The issue as to what should be published is taken up later since it raises ethical issues. Let it just be acknowledged here that there are issues regarding the reporting unit but also the problem arises that the vocabulary of research includes words that raise anxieties such as: 'negative', 'below average' and 'regression'.

Tymms has suggested that a drift in standards seems to be characteristic in national tests in English primary schools. The reasons for this are connected with the practice of piloting items and setting their difficulty from the results on students who knew they were simply taking an exercise. This 'adrenaline-free' un-prepared testing situation might produce lower performance that would then serve as the benchmark against which the exams were calibrated the following year.

Taken under genuine examination conditions, with revision time having been invested and the adrenaline flowing, students might well be producing much better results than those calibrated. Hence the unconscious drift in 'standards'. It is an unusual teacher-training course that prepares teachers for the kind of information that is now available in England through professional monitoring systems. And yet the information is now seen as vital to many educational professionals.

In the course of setting up the CEM Centre projects' sessions to explain the feedback and to discuss the implications. Further, many courses have been run locally for schools to understand and use the data. The enormous need for in-service work is an essential part of any monitoring system and that the extent of the need for conferences and workshops often only becomes apparent as the project starts running.

A school may implement an innovation and the indicator suggests worse results But perhaps the results would have been even worse without the innovation. Who knows? So the school repeats the innovation and the results stay the same. So another year's data are awaited—and so on. If instead of this year by year indicator monitoring, if a school joined with 20 other schools and a random 10 implemented one innovation and the other random half implemented a different innovation, all schools would receive 20 years of data in one year. By adopting the methods of science, learning is speeded up and made more reliable.

Epidemiology and clinical trials both have their virtues, but the clinical trials are necessary to establish sound evidence as to what works. That concept applies in education as in medicine and the term 'evidence-based' is now becoming popular.

As 'value-added' became the popular word for residuals, evidence-based may become the popular word for experiments. A major ethical imperative is to do good rather than to do harm. At the very least we might try to observe the Hippocratic oath and 'at least do no harm'.

Evidence of the likely impact of indicator systems on participating schools will be considered including the small number of controlled trials that exist. In addition to this question about the overall impact of indicators there are numerous ethical issues to be addressed that arise in the course of running indicator systems.

The effect of the randomly assigned feedback was measured not against no feedback but against already substantial feedback, so to expect any further improvement was perhaps optimistic. Nevertheless as a result of giving classroom by classroom analyses to the teachers concerned, rather than simply departmental data from which this information could be extracted. In the

Years Late Secondary Information System, a list of under-aspiring students is produced by combining students' intentions regarding continuing in education with their baseline scores.

Many schools given the list of under-aspiring students set up mentoring sessions or special monitoring. Unfortunately, good intentions do not guarantee good outcomes. Aware of the ethical responsibility not to have teachers wasting their time and in order to avoid harming students, we obtained permission from some schools to only feed back to them a random half of the list of their under-aspiring students.

In following up these schools and comparing the outcomes of the named under-aspirers versus the unnamed under-aspirers, we actually have found more differences in favour of the unnamed group than the named group. Only 15 schools were involved in this first experiment, but it calls into question many facile beliefs about how achievement can be improved.

The findings are challenging and the experiment is being repeated with thirty schools. It illustrates how an indicator system can move the profession forward to proper experimentation. The resistance to a National Curriculum in the U.S. has contributed to the slow development of curriculum-embedded, high-stakes, authentic tests.

In England, where external curriculum-embedded assessments have been used for decades and school performance tables are published using raw results, moves have been made towards value added systems. These will increase the high stakes nature of the external examinations and, at the same time, government pressure on the Qualifications and Curriculum Authority has led to a reduction from seven independent examination boards to three conglomerates of the former boards.

Furthermore there has been a reduction in the number of syllabuses on offer for secondary schools. Meanwhile in primary schools, a single National Curriculum has been imposed and all primary students sit the same tests designed to the same syllabuses at the ages of 7, 11 and 14 years. The specification of a National Curriculum concentrating on particular subjects and the publication of these data has put schools under pressure to drop attention to such areas as the fine arts, the performing arts, and physical education, and to concentrate on those indicators that are published. All schools are forced to do the same curriculum unless exemptions are granted. This restriction and concentration certainly represents a downgrading of the professional status of teachers who can now make few important decisions, and it may contribute to declining levels of satisfaction of teachers.

At the very least there should be various curricula available to be chosen, as was the case for decades for teachers of students aged 16 and 18 years. Thus, a teacher who preferred to teach physical geography rather than economic geography could find a syllabus in which the proportion was attractive for that teacher. Another reason for maintaining choice and diversity in syllabuses is that in the entire population a much broader range of skills is thereby likely to be developed.

Choice and diversity also keep the examination boards in competition and this ought to lead to an improvement in the quality of the service that they provide. Unfortunately, since they have a virtual monopoly endowed by government approval, it will not be likely that examination boards drop their poor practice unless required to do so.

Examples of poor practice from examination boards are leaving the names of students and their schools on the examination paper when it is being assessed. The name of the pupil and the school will often contain clear evidence regarding the pupil's gender, ethnicity, social class and religion. There may be differences between groups, but ethnicity is very poorly defined; socio-economic status is not well-measured; and neither of these variables, is alterable by the school.

Religion is perhaps an alterable variable, but Catholic schools are doing better than Protestant schools. The habit of analysing by these unalterable variables may simply be a result of the pressure to produce academic papers, whether they contribute to practical or theoretical developments or not. Given a body of data it is easy to break it down by these categories, and report the differences. The fact that it leads nowhere has not been a major consideration in social science research. The fact that such analyses perpetuate stereotyping should also be a matter of ethical concern.

That these correlational analyses do not promote the search for strong evidence as to what works, is certainly a matter for ethical concern. Attention should be directed towards alterable variables rather than unalterable categories into which human beings are grouped, which is the first step to stereotyping. These analyses become particularly a matter of concern when teachers are presumed to be somehow to blame for the 'under-achievement' of boys at the age of 16 as compared with the achievement of girls.

Group differences make catchy headlines in the newspapers. While there may sometimes be a need to track group differences, there is a more important need to educate users of data about the size of the effects being studied and what is known about altering the situation.

At the secondary level the damaging and unethical impact is a concentration on D students because the reporting line is the percentage of students getting Grade C or above. Time, effort and money have been spent on D students to the neglect of more able and less able students. If, on the other hand, an average points score is used as the outcome measure, the implication is to work with each pupil to obtain their maximum performance.

In England, official bodies such as the Office for Standards in Education, lacking pupil level value added measures, compare schools with 'similar' schools. The classification of 'similar' is usually made on the basis of the percent of students receiving free school meals. However, two schools can both have 20 per cent of students receiving free school meals but otherwise have quite different profiles.

For example, one may have a larger proportion of children who also come from schools with very high levels of achievement. Such a school benchmarked against a school with the same percent of free school meals will look very good at the expense of the other school, but the comparison is spurious. Such benchmarking is an inadequate way of making comparisons. The only fair comparisons are with similar students in other schools. It is certainly not ethical to make unfair comparisons which in some cases carry financial consequences for the institution concerned and can lead to job losses and demoralisation. Indeed, to take a most extreme and serious consequence, Ofsted inspectors rely on poor benchmarking data and also sit in classrooms judging teachers.

In short, whole school indicators should be avoided because the evidence is that there is more variation within a single school than is generally found between schools. Furthermore, the use of whole school indicators encourages the rank ordering of schools and the public is not prepared to interpret rank orders adequately.

Very small differences in the indicator can move a school through many positions in a rank ordering in the middle of a distribution. If indicators were published for each teacher, this would be tantamount to doing personnel work in public and would be unacceptable. And yet data cannot be withheld from the public unreasonably, so some compromise is needed: not whole school indicators and not individual teacher indicators.

In small schools there may be no distinction between the indicators for a curriculum area and for a teacher. There needs to be some restriction put on the size of sample that can be reported publicly. The CEM Centre is developing these indicators for the provision of data at the LEA10/School District level as opposed to individual school level, where the data is presented department by department for affective and cognitive indicators, and student by student in the cognitive area. Within the individual school, further analyses can be undertaken to obtain data teacher by teacher.

Mistaken beliefs about the nature of the physical world have no influence on the physical world, but distortions of beliefs about the social world can have an impact. One of the distortions promulgated by those seeking to implement performance related pay is that pay is the great motivator. This is only a hypothesis, and before huge amounts of money go into implementing performance related pay systems, they should be put to an experimental test in which some schools get performance related pay and other schools get equivalent money to spend as they wish.

The negative influences of performance related pay are potentially the destruction of team work, the demoralisation of those who do not get a performance pay rise, the corruption of data due to the chance to make financial gain from 'good' exam results, and the message sent to students that teachers work for pay: not for their love of the subject, not for their concern for their students, but for pay.

Indicator systems, feasible because of computers, may make the public sector, and in particular public sector management, a fascinating exercise in applied social science. Finally social scientists may have some responsibility for more than arguments and papers. The actions of managers and administrators should be guided by social science findings.

They can study their success in applying the findings by watching the indicators as business managers watch the bottom line or the share price. Perhaps indeed the pensions of Chief Education Officers could be tied to the long-term outcomes of the students who are in their care for about 15,000 hours of compulsory treatment.

Educational Technology and Teritary Education in South East Asia

The New Frontiers, New Technologies, New Pedagogies

research project is a preliminary investigation of the ways in which information and communication technology are internationalising education in, and the socio-cultural implications of these developments. In the digital age, educational materials, whether supplemental course materials or whole online courses, are able to transcend geographical barriers. The frontiers of higher education institutions are no longer defined by commuting distances or national boundaries. Instead, their reach is now more fluid, and is increasingly shaped by the local availability of communications technologies, language skills, commonalities of interest and un-met demand in far off places. Informational and communication technologies are transforming the ways in which teachers teach and students learn. An insight into the issues that arise at the intersection of these changes, when new frontiers, new technologies and new pedagogies meet. Focusing on developments in Singapore, Malaysia and Vietnam, it explores some of the sociocultural implications of the internationalisation that results from the use of new technologies in higher education.

The project was funded by Telstra Australia and carried out by the Monash Centre for Research in International Education. It is intended to form a basis for discussion in the field and to assist in planning future research projects on the specific issues identified and to inform the development of more culturally reflexive uses of educational technologies in international contexts.

The Digital Divide

The use of educational technology is significantly altering access to higher education. New technologies are lessening geographical barriers to education. Individuals and institutions with access to the Internet have an enormous volume of educational materials at their disposal, regardless of their physical location. However, such access comes at a price, and the need for expensive hardware, software and telecommunications poses a serious financial barrier for much of the population of the region.

Academics in poor countries such as Vietnam are beginning to obtain Internet access, which allows them to keep up to date with international developments in the field, access publications and maintain international networks of colleagues. This requirement is increasing infrastructure costs for educational institutions, which is particularly difficult for public institutions in poor countries. This also creates new barriers to entry for prospective students, who are increasingly required to have independent access to computer equipment and Internet access. The geographical centre-periphery divide in education is slowly being replaced by a digital divide between those who can afford to participate in global information networks and those who cannot.

The use of information and communication technologies in education is expanding access to information, educational products and whole courses, which are coming to form a globalised information network. Access to these technologies is a precondition for participation in a global information society. Clearly, individuals and institutions that are able to access and participated in these global networks are at an advantage. However, there are, of course, huge disparities in access to information and communications technologies. In recent years, inequalities in access to new information and communications technologies have become increasingly apparent.

On a global scale, the cosmopolitanism of the wealthy is in stark contrast to the localism of the poor. With economic globalisation, increasingly the wealthy have ready access to global communications media, work for companies with branches in many countries, have colleagues and clients from different cultural backgrounds, travel regularly for business and pleasure, and generally think, feel and act transnationally. (Castells 1989) The groups which are 'information rich' in the sense that they have ready access to information and communications technology, also possess a worldview that is disembedded enough from the particularities of local conditions to allow them to traverse the cultural differences of a global arena with relative ease. In wealthier societies, such as Australia, the United States and Singapore, a large proportion of the population have access to such networks. Public education systems in these countries are connected to global flows of information, albeit with inferior machines and lower bandwidth than the private education sector. In poorer countries, much smaller segments of the popular are able to participate. Public education systems are stretched providing more basic services across the country, while private education institutions offer those who can afford it an entry point into the global information society.

The Digital Divide in the United States

The United States have detailed the extent of inequalities in access to computers and the Internet in that country. Even within wealthy societies such as the United States, there is a clear relationship between socioeconomic status, computer ownership and Internet access. This is not to imply that one can draw a neat line between those with computers and online and those without computers and offline. Nevertheless, whether socioeconomic status is measured according to income, race or educational attainment, the same patterns appear-socially advantaged groups are also technologically advantaged. This is to be expected, but the implications of this distribution for the equity and access to online education, and for the character of the emerging markets in educational services have been largely ignored by educational institutions.

The American College Board concludes that 'the result of the new technologies may be to deepen the divide between educational haves and have-nots, and that the marketplace alone will not fix the problem. Public policy must intervene to narrow the 'digital divide' between whites and minorities, the wealthy and the less advantaged.' These inequalities are not likely to be addressed by the market because educational providers are currently competing to attract those students who can afford the technology and enrolment fees to their new courses.

International Disparities in Access to Educational Technology: On an international level, the inequalities are starker, as are the implications. Within a nation, governments can be persuaded that they have a responsibility to ensure fairer access to new media in education. For example, in the United States the Clinton government has taken steps to provide financial aid to ensure public access to groups who cannot afford to privately acquire the technology. In addition to egalitarian concerns, there is a strong national economic imperative driving this effort to provide broad access to learning technology. Similar policies have been adopted by most wealthy nations, as much out of eagerness to universalise the reach of emerging technologies, expand their high-tech industries and train a large high-tech labour force as out of a concern with educational equality. In the international arena, however, there are no equivalent transnational entities that have the ability to redress inequalities in access to technology to provide wider access to the fruits of the Information Age.

Much of the world's population do not have access to the most basic communication technologies, such as postal services and telephones, either because these are not available, not reliable or are prohibitively expensive. In less technologically developed regions, differentials in access to information and communication technologies are stark. While a small number of educational institutions are benefiting from the introduction of new technologies, the majority who do not have access find themselves further behind than they were before. For example, in Malaysia, while the Smart Schools program brings Internet connections and online teaching materials to a select group of schools, many remote primary schools across the country are still without telephones. Rather than broadening access to education, the incorporation of educational technologies seems to be reproducing existing inequalities. Especially in poorer societies, there is a marked difference between the private, internationalised sector and the national public sector.

Vietnam is the poorest and least technologically developed of the three countries considered in this study, having an average per capita income of just USD200 per annum, which is much lower than Singapore and Malaysia. Vietnam has been connected to the Internet only since November 1997, but its use in education is developing rapidly. In mid 1999, there were around 30,000 Internet subscribers in Vietnam. To give some indication of the rate of growth, the largest Internet Service Provider, the Vietnam Datacommunication Company, has over 18,000 subscribers, of which 7,733 joined in the first half of 1999. Significantly, foreigners hold around one third of Internet accounts in Vietnam, while comprising a tiny fraction of the population. Government agencies and business enterprises hold one quarter of all accounts and individuals hold the remainder. Many institutional subscribers have many individual users.

At the other end of the spectrum, Singapore has the highest standard of living in South East Asia. The government of Singapore is looking to make the country a global hub for e-commerce as a way to maintain economic growth in the wake of the Asian financial crisis. The government estimated in 1998 that e-commerce transactions in Singapore would total USD150 million by the end of that year. In recent years there has been considerable government investment in technology infrastructure. In a recent survey of IT infrastructure investment in 55 countries, Singapore was ranked fourth in the world, behind the United States, Sweden and Finland. Singapore had 394,000 dial-up Internet subscribers in 1998, or around 10% of the population. Other estimates put total Internet access (dial-up, work and school) at 17 percent of the population in 1998 but these figures are increasing rapidly.

In early 2000, the Singapore government announced a three-year initiative intended to make the country one of the top five information societies in the world, in terms of rates of Internet use and home PC ownership. These will be coordinated by the Infocomm Development Authority and include such measures as providing free e-mail address and Web pages for all citizens over five years of age and distributing 30,000 used computers with software, modems and free Internet access to low-income households. Such measures are explicitly intended to overcome the digital divide and have the potential to significantly reduce barriers to access for poor students.

Singapore has long been using educational technology. Since independence in 1965, educational television has been used to support classroom teaching. In response to the current national IT agenda, the Ministry of Education has developed an IT Masterplan, a comprehensive strategy that aims to integrate information technology throughout the educational system.

The philosophy of the Masterplan is that:

> *education should continually anticipate the future needs of society, and work towards fulfilling those needs. The skills required for the future will centre on thinking skills, learning skills and communication skills. IT-based teaching and learning will be one of key strategies for equipping young with these skills.*

By 2002, the Masterplan aims to achieve a pupil to computer ratio of 2:1 in schools and aims to have students spending 30 per cent of their school time in IT-based curriculum. The government is also encouraging local universities and polytechnics to incorporate IT in educational delivery. The Singapore One broadband network offers educational institutions a means of delivering audio and video intensive multimedia to Singaporean students.

The peripheries of the global information society

In recent years, educational institutions' spending on

information and communications technology has increased dramatically around the world. Within developed societies like the United States, wealthier educational institutions are making greatest use of new media while poorer ones lag behind. While wealthier institutions in developed countries are using ICTs for course delivery, flexibility and interaction at a distance, in poorer institutions in developing countries, computers are still primarily used for teaching computer science and computer literacy.

The public universities in Vietnam are the most poorly resourced of the institutions visited for this study. When viewed in historical context, however, the facilities are improving dramatically. A Faculty Dean at Hanoi Open University recounted to us how 30 years ago he would bring suitcases full of books back from overseas, which would then be copied manually. 'In my time, I have copied by hand several books of about four or five hundred pages. We had no facilities such as photocopiers and so on.' It was common for books to be translated into Vietnamese in this way. Manuscripts would be distributed to students, who separated them into many parts and copied the parts by hand to distribute to others.

Staff who studied overseas return and teach students how to use the Internet and e-mail. The university is beginning to put content on to the Web, but only a few subjects are using the Web so far. Curriculum has changed in IT courses because lecturers have incorporated elements from course descriptions and lecture notes found on the Web. Students access to information is changing rapidly, especially in IT courses. First-year IT students are now required to do some research using online resources and new subjects being developed use the Internet more than existing ones. Theses submitted in the past year commonly include URLs in bibliography, and all theses submitted at HCMUT are now available online.

When the University first began to gain access to the Internet between 1995 and 1997, it was only available to academic staff members in the faculty of information technology. Even this restricted access was very costly to the institution, whose 64 Kbps bandwidth Internet access cost more then the combined salaries of the 40 academic staff in the IT Faculty. In 1998, the IT faculty developed a network connecting 14 higher education institutions in Ho Chi Minh City. These institutions now have a 256 Kbps bandwidth connection to the Internet through the network. Now, all staff and students in Ho Chi Minh City University of Technology and these other institutions have freely available Internet access.

In contrast, the better-resourced private institutions in Vietnam, such as the Asian Institute of Technology Centre in Vietnam (AITCV) use technology more extensively, but are out of reach of most students. The majority of students at such private institutions rely on financial support from outside, which the institution tries to organise through grants from governments and corporations. Some bigger corporations that are in need of human resource fund scholarships to AITCV. As one lecturer noted, 'from the student's perspective the AITCV education is quite expensive, compared to the income level. So, more or less, people are expecting that they'll get a scholarship otherwise they won't be able to attend.' AITCV's ability to provide computer labs and Internet access in a poor country like Vietnam is dependent upon such support from international corporations and foreign governments. Public universities in Malaysia have access to more resources than their Vietnamese equivalents but use educational technologies to a much lesser extent than the new Malaysian private universities. Public universities are focusing their energies on providing adequate computer laboratories. Enrolments at public universities in Malaysia have increased dramatically in recent years, due both to the financial crisis, which has prevented some students from studying overseas, and the Malaysian government's commitment to increase the proportion of the population in higher education.

Between 1997 and 1999, the annual intake of the country's eight public universities increased from 45,000 to 84,000 students. This is a dramatic change in enrolments that, of itself, would put great pressure on any institution. The crisis in pubic universities has been compounded by severe funding cuts. As a result, facilities in public universities are stretched at present and there is little resources available for investment in educational technology. These institutions cannot expect that their students are able to afford their own hardware. While PC ownership in Malaysia is currently restricted to the middle-class, there is a sense that computers and Internet access are becoming more affordable for most Malaysians. As one lecturer told us, at this point PC ownership becomes a question of priorities for many people.

Integrating academics into global networks

The Internet allows for far more constant and ongoing relationships to be established between lecturers and researchers in different countries. In academia, the Internet has become a necessity for inclusion and participation in contemporary global networks. As the management and production of information becomes ever more central to contemporary capitalism, the divide between inclusion and exclusion in the global flows of information become more crucial. Many academics in South East Asia are only slowly gaining entry to these networks, as the infrastructure is put in place and as the content of online academic interchange becomes less centred on activities in the United States. While most academics in Malaysia now have Internet connections, very few academics in Vietnam do, and these tend to be foreign nationals working in transnational institutions or ICT specialists working in computer science departments in public institutions.

Universities have always been relatively internationalised workplaces, and many academic staff will have studied or worked in another country at some stage in their career. In developing countries, it is common for a majority of academics to have received a large part of their education in developed countries. Many of the lecturers in the universities visited were educated in American and British Universities. As one lecturer in a Malaysian university explained, lecturers bring back what they have learnt in these countries and adapt it to local conditions.

As well as bringing back knowledge from abroad which is then adapted to local conditions, this experience creates international linkages which the lecturers continue to develop upon their return. International postgraduate study-Masters and Doctoral programs-which many lecturers in Malaysia, Singapore and Vietnam have experienced, often establishes ongoing research, publishing and teaching connections. Opportunities for international colleagues to meet face-to-face are infrequent, and in the past, such networks were largely maintained by letter-writing and occasional phone calls. Now, e-mail has allowed these international collaborations to be maintained on a day-to-day basis much more easily.

Internet access is helping Vietnamese universities participate in global academic networks. In the past lecturers would bring back suitcases full of books on their return to Vietnam. Now they order books and download articles online. The IT department subscribes online to The American Computer Magazine and IEEE International Electronic Engineering. They now have faster access to international information technology developments. Staff now obtain international scholarship and grant information online and can apply for these directly. In past students and academics had to rely on the government to organise these. They have established international relationships with particular lecturers overseas who organise funding and exchanges. At a private transnational provider in Vietnam, like AIT, the communications infrastructure now means that they are as connected to global networks as any other institution in the world. As one AIT lecturer noted, 'in terms of someone working at the institution having access to the world, there's no difference I guess between AIT and many other places around the world.'

Students' access to computers

Educational providers must now decide whether they will require their students to provide their own computer and Internet access. Many universities in the most technologically advanced societies now require their students to provide their own a computer and Internet access, and this is also beginning to be a requirement in private universities in Malaysia.

Public distance education providers in South East Asia cannot expect their students to have access to computers and the Internet. The Hanoi Open University, for example, estimates that only 10 per cent of their students have PCs. While distance education in Australia and other developed societies has usually required students to provide their own equipment, in South East Asia distance education has relied on study centres to provide various facilities and face-to-face teaching. The GNP per capita in Ho Chi Minh City is only a little more than US$1000 per year. The GNP in Hanoi is about US$800. This makes computer equipment very expensive. Connection fees for the Internet are very high in comparison with other countries. Internet fees, like international telephony and postage rates, are very expensive by local standards. In 1999, Internet access and installation charges were cut by up to 50 percent on 1998 prices. There are different rates for government officials and general users.

Two Malaysian private universities that were visited in this study-the International Medical University and UNITAR-are strongly encouraging their students to purchase personal computers. UNITAR has its own IT shop that sells desktop computers and notebooks at special prices for UNITAR students through a deal between the institution and a manufacturer.

The university provides finance so that students can purchase a PC with a small deposit and regular monthly payments. Because UNITAR's viability is reliant on students owning computers, it wants to ensure there are minimal barriers to its students owning PCs. UNITAR argues that the money students save in commuting costs and lower fees should be put towards purchasing a PC. IMU is also entering into an agreement with a hardware supplier to decrease costs to its students. It is planning to move to a new building in which it will provide numerous

Internet access points for notebook computers rather than traditional computer labs.

From September 1999, new students must provide their own notebook computer. UTUM would also like to see their students migrate onto the net, but considers that this is not a realistic expectation of all students in the short term both due to financial constraints and poor telecommunications infrastructure in some places. However, the university believes that nearly all students at UTUM-which is a private university that specialises in technology courses-already have access to the net. Likewise, Monash University Malaysia estimates that 80 per cent of its Malaysian students have computers at home. The level technology infrastructure at these institutions seems comparable to most Australian universities.

Expanding access through distance education

Across South East Asia, governments have encouraged public universities to use distance education to deliver low-cost mass education. Distance education providers such as Universitas Terbuka in Indonesia, Universiti Sains Malaysia and Hanoi Open University have expanded access to higher education for students in outlying areas and for working adults. These institutions are slowly integrating new technologies into teaching and learning, but are hampered by their students' lack of access to computer equipment and because they lack the significant funds required for such innovation. Meanwhile, new privately-owned entrants into the distance education market such as UNITAR are capitalising on the promise of online education, painting themselves as virtual universities.

Distance education can be offered with varying levels of student support. In most cases, printed learning materials and text books are sent to the students. Increasingly, CD-ROMs, videos and the World Wide Web are being used to supplement these printed resources. When discussing distance education internationally, it is important to distinguish between 'remotely-supported' and 'locally-supported' distance education. Remotely-supported distance education is delivered to students who study independently and have little face-to-face contact with teaching staff and other students. This is common in Australia and in some other Western countries but rare in South East Asia. Much more common is locally-supported distance education, in which a local study centre provides various services to students, from tutorial support to library facilities.

This may involve short-term visits by lecturers or tutors from a central campus or ongoing teaching from locally recruited staff who are able to contextualise centrally-produced teaching materials. Most transnational distance education providers contract local partners to provide a range of services to students. Increasingly, institutions are providing students with access to tutors via the Internet, using e-mail, discussion forums and on-line tutorials.

The three distance education providers visited-University Sains Malaysia, Hanoi Open University and TMC-all used local study centres to provide the hardware required by students at these locations rather than requiring students to have such equipment at home. A similar situation exists in Hong Kong, where distance education students are heavily reliant on computer facilities and workspaces provided by the institution.

Hanoi open university

The Hanoi Open University (HOU) was opened in 1993 as a dual mode university, offering both on-campus and distance education, with the aim of broadening access to tertiary education in Vietnam. Having opened its borders to international markets in recent years, Vietnam faced a need for specialists in many areas of the new internationalised economy. The government hoped to meet these needs with the establishment of two open universities and by encouraging continuing education. There are currently around 50,000 students enrolled in distance education at university level in Vietnam, most of whom are studying at the HOU, the Ho Chi Minh City Semi-Public Open University or Hue University. HOU currently has around 32,000 students, of which half are distance students, quarter full-time on-campus students and quarter part-time on-campus students. The language of instruction is Vietnamese.

The demographics of distance education in Vietnam are similar to those in other countries. While most of HOU's full-time students are school-leavers, most distance students are working and many have previous degrees. As a HOU administrator explained, working adults 'want to take distance education so that they can be working and they can be learning at the same time. And, for example, if they are busy this month and they can not take the test or exam, maybe next month or the month after next they will come for the test or the examination again.' HOU has 12 local study centres across Vietnam for distance students, who are located all over the country, including remote and mountainous areas. Tutors and lecturers visit these at regular times to conduct tutorials, revision classes, tests and examinations in conjunction with teachers based at the local study centre. HOU allows students to study without attending the local study centres but few do in practice. Teaching materials are mostly in printed form, supplemented by video and audio tapes, television and radio programs. HOU plans to put computers in use for distance education and has developed its own Intranet, which it plans to put to use for distance education. At present, students use the audio and video programs both at home and at study centres.

Those who have access to television and radio at home can watch or listen to programs as they are broadcast on Vietnam National Radio and Vietnam National Television. Others can watch or listen to those programs on tape at the local study centre. Use of computer-based delivery would be organised similarly, with both home and study-centre access. HOU is establishing an intranet called 'Open Net' to connect learning centers around the country. This will be used for centralised administration and management, dissemination of materials and communications between staff and students. It will use a satellite connection between campuses, which is cheaper than Internet connection and faster. The development of an intranet and the Internet at HOU, will follow the same model, and students will continue to be heavily reliant on facilities provided by the institution at study centres.

Universiti Sains Malaysia

Universiti Sains Malaysia (USM), Malaysia's largest and longest-serving provider of distance education, has 20 regional learning centres across the country, which provide administrative support, face-to-face teaching, resources and, increasingly, access to teleconferencing suites and computer equipment. Videoconferencing has been used extensively in recent years for the delivery of lectures to these learning centres. Because of budget cuts in Malaysian public universities, USM has a limited capacity to develop applications of information and communications technologies in distance education. Fees for distance education students at USM are very low-around RM 1,000 (US$265) per year, or RM 3,000 (US$790) for a full three year degree-so there is little revenue from distance education directly. Nevertheless, USM is now moving to put all distance education teaching materials online so that students can access resources from computer labs in the regional learning centres or from computers connected to the Internet at home or work.

The gradual adoption of online delivery and Internet connectivity by these public distance education providers will provide students with access to international online resources. However their languages of instruction-Vietnamese and Bahasa Malaysia respectively-limit the extent to which external online resources can be used in teaching and learning. Students at such institutions cannot be expected to be able to work with English-language materials, which currently make up the vast majority of online resources.

TMC centre for advanced seminars (Singapore)

The TMC Centre for Advanced Seminars in Singapore administers distance education courses for Monash University, Deakin University, the University of Newcastle and the University of London as well as offering its own short and diploma courses. Since the currency crisis, the demand for foreign university courses delivered in Singapore has increased dramatically. Students who would previously have travelled to study abroad are opting to do courses offered in Singapore by international institutions.

There is little regulation of distance education courses in Singapore as long as no face-to-face teaching is provided. However, there is a need to inform the Ministry of Education of the collaborative arrangement, including submission of course contents. While not providing any actual teaching, TMC provides a range of other services to students enrolled in international distance programs, including advertising and information sessions for prospective students, orientation programs, administrative support, study group meeting sessions, student support and counselling, local submission of assignments and library facilities.

Before the Internet, TMC students had fax and postal access to their overseas lecturers, and students were issued with a fax allowance for use of the TMC fax machine. Since 1995, TMC have provided students with access to Internet facilities so they can contact lecturers via e-mail, participate in discussion forums, conduct research and submit assignments online.

Students are increasingly interacting with teaching staff from the foreign universities via online a-synchronous conference sessions, especially in computing and communications courses. But even with such online interaction, according to TMC, students still value local facilities and face-to-face support highly, and there is little demand for courses taught online without such support.

Virtual Universities

The term 'virtual university' is usually reserved for institutions that have no campus and teach students exclusively by distance mode using educational technologies. This is perhaps the most intensive application of educational technologies into higher education, evidenced in the United States by universities such as Jones International University. In a technical sense, relying on Internet-based communication allows the institution to operate globally. In the earlier print/post phase of remotely-supported distance education, most students tended to live near the institution, and almost entirely within the same country. Internationalisation was difficult due to the cost, slowness and unreliability of international communications. By using e-mail and the Web, it is now possible for prospective students to choose from a wide range of courses offered by providers based in many different nations. However, in practice, online universities appear to draw most of their students from within their home country. A number of online universities have begun to market themselves internationally, including Jones International and the University of Southern Queensland.

Two institutions in the countries visited refer to themselves as virtual universities. The differences between them offer some indication of the ways in which this organisational form may be applied in South East Asia. Universiti Tun Abdul Razak (UNITAR) UNITAR is a private university in Malaysia founded in 1998 that set out to be a 'virtual' university with no physical campus, relying entirely on technologically-mediated communications.

When the university was first proposed, the Malaysia Education Minister expressed concern about the lack of socialisation in remotely-supported distance education. In short, UNITAR was told: 'no socialisation, no education, no license, no operation'. In response, the virtual university model was altered, requiring compulsory attendance at local study centres in all subjects. In the first semester, attendance is required for 22 hours per subject and in subsequent semesters students must attend eight hours of classes per subject. UNITAR has had to establish a network of local learning centres, which students can attend for classes, interaction, exams and access to computers and support. These are very similar to the learning centres of established distance education providers, but with more reliance on educational technologies.

Due to the cost and unreliability of dial-up Internet connections in Malaysia, which were then prone to drop-outs and low bandwidth, UNITAR decided to distribute teaching materials to students on CD-ROMs. Students are required to go online to access the library, complete administrative tasks, participate in forums and tutorials. UNITAR established a courseware team consisting of 120 instructional designers, multimedia programmers, graphic designers and audio-visual producers. They work with lecturers and module writers, most of whom are employed on contract.

UNITAR's online content is primarily text-based, including answers to common questions from students, which are compiled into a FAQ (frequently asked questions) list. Threaded discussion forums display only the last week's messages, encouraging students to read and respond regularly. Virtual tutorials are held once or twice each month, using chat, a shared whiteboard and Real Audio. UNITAR has a virtual library (as well as a small physical library on their KL campus) which holds 3,000 titles, mainly online journals. UNITAR responds to students requests and complaints through a call centre. This forwards queries on to the appropriate person by e-mail, and they should respond within 24 hours.

The university prides itself on making use of academic staff time more efficiently than other tertiary institutions by minimizing research activities and standardizing course content to minimise differences between lecturing staff. Lecturers are supposed to respond to student inquiries within 24 hours, and if the student receives no response within 48 hours, the lecturer's supervisor is notified.

UNITAR intends to launch campuses in Singapore and in the south of the Philippines, and later in several Middle-Eastern countries. Their international activities also extend to providing focusing on educational technology solutions and consultancy services for the region. The intent to work with schools, universities and virtual learning providers, both in content development and course delivery.

TMC is part owner of a Singapore-based online education company, CyberCampus 21, which hosts online courses and provides related technical and educational services. These services include providing hardware, software and support services to both educational providers and users. CyberCampus 21 currently offers an online course that is taught by TMC and a Diploma in Business Administration and Marketing that is validated by Staffordshire University on a pilot run basis. They also offer two short courses called Servesafe Food Safety

Program Writing Right: An Introductory Course to the Basics of Writing Well. TMC sees the online study option provided by CyberCampus 21 as one of a range of different delivery options, which their students can choose between. TMC plan to use CyberCampus 21 to offer a range of international courses in much the same way as they offer distance education courses. Online content would be provided by the international university and TMC would provide local marketing, administration, face-to-face teaching and student support.

These two institutions provide examples of two different types of 'virtual' university. UNITAR operates in a similar way to existing universities, developing and teaching its own courses, but the majority of its teaching and learning is done through computers. CyberCampus 21, by contrast, does not develop its own content but operates as a hosting service for the online components of distance education courses developed by other institutions.

While all the distance education providers visited in the course of this study were moving to incorporate educational technology, none were moving away from also providing face-to-face teaching and support to students. There appeared to be no significant demand for remotely supported distance education. As in other parts of the world, online courses seem to be most popular with working adults seeking postgraduate qualifications, especially in business and information technology. For undergraduate students, the lack of on-campus socialisation appears to be a significant disincentive.

Educational Technologies and the Internationalisation of Curriculum

'Wired' students can, in theory, access material produced

remotely as easily as material produced locally. The ability to access the Internet on campus has the potential to lift students out of a local face-to-face context and connect them with a global informational sphere. In this way, educational technologies are globalising the production and consumption of information, so that the same types of information are increasingly available to university lecturers and students anywhere in the wired world.

At the same time, however, educational technologies appear to be speeding up the homogenisation of knowledge production and dissemination around the world, resulting in the devaluation of local cultures and local knowledges. Among the educators interviewed in this study, the Internet was widely seen as promoting the standardisation of curriculum on a global scale. These educators considered themselves adept at taking what was locally useful from the proliferation of online materials. These lecturers play a significant role in mediating between the producers and users of online materials, framing and interpreting the content to make it useful for their students.

On an international level, the connection of higher education institutions to the Internet furthers the standardisation of knowledge, teaching and learning. While educational technology may provide students with a larger number of online courses to choose from, it is likely that all these choices will become increasingly similar over time. In the world of networked computing, the forces of institutional isomorphism are amplified greatly.' Isomorphism here refers to the tendency of institutions to become increasingly similar through imitatation of each others' ideas, practices and organisational structures. The used of information and communication technologies in education has enhances these processes in several ways:

— The management of different institutions and different parts of the same institution must be standardised in order to be integrated into overarching computerised networks.

— The trend towards modularity, whereby students can combine subjects offered by different providers to constitute a degree, is fuelled by the increased availability of information about courses and the trend towards distance delivery. In order to respond to governments' and students' desires for greater inter-institutional mobility, universities are under pressure to standardise offerings in line with other providers.

— Greater interaction and cooperation between educators around the globe may result in less diversity in their teaching, research and publishing rather than more.

— The standardisation of computerised systems and software allows for much greater portability of educational materials, resulting in global markets for educational texts, courseware applications and multimedia programs. For example, electronic journals and online book purchasing are fuelling of the globalisation of academic publishing.

Because of the dominance of the English language in the digital realm, educational technologies put additional pressure on those aiming to maintain linguistic diversity in education. English language skills become increasingly important for students, and cultural producers in English-speaking countries have a rapidly increasing audience around the globe.

The globalisation of knowledge

In the past, universities saw themselves as a place apart, to quote the title of a recent history of the University of Melbourne. They strived to maintain and develop bodies of knowledge developed in Europe's elite institutions by operating independently, disembedded from their local contexts. In this sense, both the form and content of modern higher education has always been international to some extent, however in a very different form to the globalisation that has occurred in the latter half of the twentieth century.

Universities have long seen science and technology as universal, culturally neutral forms of knowledge. These disciplines have been taught globally with little regard for local differences. Through the spread of Western education around the world, these forms of knowledge have become globally dominant while local knowledge, skills and cultures are often overlooked. Some writers draw attention to the ways in which the dominant forms of Western science have appropriated elements of knowledge systems from around the globe and combined them to develop a coherent world-view. In this way, science can be de-Westernised, and made more relevant to non-Western students by teaching about the diverse cultural roots of science. This does not seem to be occurring widely in practice, and the tendency is more commonly for local knowledges to be treated as inferior to bodies of knowledge imported from the most technologically advanced post-industrial societies.

While science and technology education are perhaps the most globalised, the internationalisation of other disciplines is also occurring. Monash University Malaysia began operation offering the more 'generic' courses-engineering, IT and business programs-which have been adapted only minimally for offshore delivery.

In any discipline, there are aspects of the curriculum that are able to be transported more readily than others. While the theoretical foundations of many social science subjects can be taught transnationally, the empirical content of humanities and social science subjects usually reflects the social environment in which these courses are taught to a far greater degree than the sciences, business and technology subjects. This lecturer explained that: in communications, when [students] are learning about what communic-ations technologies are and can be and how they are located, we give them Raymond Williams-a British writer whose thinking has driven cultural studies critiques of technology for about 30 years. And they could apply that to here. While the specific content of such courses may vary according to the local social context, it is likely that similar theoretical approaches will guide knowledge production and teaching in very different societies. There was general agreement amongst participants in this study that 'the influence of context differs from one discipline to another', as one interviewee put it.

Economic globalisation

Vocational disciplines are increasingly having global appeal as certain types of work become globally standardised. With the globalisation of capitalism, systems of production, consumption, communications and transportation are becoming increasingly standardised around the globe, making globalised training possible in those areas of life which have become most standardised. The more the process of economic globalization deepens, the more the inter-penetration of networks of production and management expands across borders, and the closer become the links between the conditions of the labor force in different countries, placed at different levels of wages and social protection, but decreasingly distinct in terms of skills and technology.' For example, the skills required to make hamburgers, fix Toyotas or use Microsoft Word do not differ markedly from one country to another. Technological globalisation has also facilitated the standardisation of tertiary education in a similar way, for example in dentistry, engineering, computer science, business administration (witness the international success of the MBA) and many other technologies.

The most internationally adaptable areas are those characterised by 'skills and concepts which are readily translatable across countries and cultures, a strong vocational emphasis, high student and/or industry demand for tailored and flexibly delivered programs and strong industry pressure for standardisation of content across institutions.'

Transnational curriculum

Transnational education, in which the institution based in a different country to its students, offers insights into the curricular issues that all tertiary education institutions will increasingly have to face in the near future. As educational materials and whole courses of study prepared in one country are used more often and more routinely by students in another part of the world, many practical issues will arise. The detail of these will vary from case to case and there is no point in trying to pre-empt them here. However, a general sketch of the responses of transnational educators is a useful starting point.

Business education and computing are the most common disciplines in international trade in education. The portability of these disciplines coincides with high demand for these skills around the world. The Internet is now essential to the operation of offshore campuses and other forms of transnational education such as international distance education. The three offshore educators visited in this study-Asian Institute of Technology Centre in Vietnam, Monash University Malaysia and TMC Educational Group, Singapore-all used Internet-based communication as their primary means of integrating their campus and their students into an international organisation. All three providers deliver courses through a combination of face-to-face teaching and technologically mediated materials. Transnational delivery usually requires that curriculum is standardised across numerous campuses located in different countries and regions, for a number of reasons:

1. Institutions achieve lower costs per student by taking advantage of the economies of scale that derive from using the same course materials (whether distributed in print, video, CD-ROM or online) for a large number of students even though they are in different locations.
2. Accreditation by host countries often requires that the course to be delivered offshore is equivalent or identical to that delivered in the home country.

3. Consistency across campuses and between partner institutions allows students to move between campuses while maintaining the continuity of their course with full course credits.

For example, the content of the Asian Institute of Technology courses taught in Hanoi is essentially the same as those taught in Bangkok, and these courses are marketed as being identical. Students studying in Hanoi must be able to transfer to the Bangkok campus with minimal disruption. Lecturers in these transnational institutions consistently that their students expect to experience a foreign education.

Some students at the Asian Institute of Technology in Hanoi (AITCV) see an international postgraduate course as a stepping stone to employment in an international corporation. Salaries in international corporations are much higher than in government organisations in Vietnam, that students expect that 'if they are accepted for AITCV then they can get good jobs in joint-venture companies.' Lecturers seemed to agree with this assessment. another saying that 'I think the program actually prepares you for international oriented type of work.' In this sense, the labour market determines the perceived appropriateness of the curriculum. That is, regardless of the actual relevance of the curriculum to the local context, the education is perceived as being valuable by employers and students. As long as international education improves students' value in the labour market, questions about the cultural and regional biases of content do not seem to concern those involved.

Transnational courses are sometimes tailored to local conditions as required, but usually only minimal modifications are made, mainly in terms of content and assignment questions. International education providers increasingly need to bridge the divide between globally- and locally-relevant education. Employers around the world now look for graduates with a balance of universal and specific knowledge, who understand local conditions but are able to work in internationalised contexts.

Asian Institute of Technology

The Asian Institute of Technology (AIT) is an international institution based in Bangkok. It was established over 40 as the South East Asian Treaty Organisation Graduate School of Engineering to serve the educational needs of the South East Asian region and it continues to be funded by many governments and foundations. It now has faculty from more than 25 countries and students from more than 40 countries. AIT has two centres in Vietnam. The AIT Centre Vietnam, located in Hanoi, was established in 1993, as the institution's first branch outside Bangkok. It provides postgraduate education, short-term training courses, language training. Vietnamese students constitute the largest group of foreign students at AIT in Bangkok. The Hanoi centre was established to provide a lower-cost alternative for Vietnamese graduate students, enabling them to complete most of their degree in Vietnam.

More recently, the Swiss-AIT-Vietnam Management Development Programme has been established at the Ho Chi Minh City University of Technology. Jointly funded by the Swiss and Vietnamese governments, this centre delivers a graduate diploma programme in Management Development to Vietnamese business lecturers from local universities and working executives. It also provides management training and support to Vietnamese companies that are in the process of restructuring prior to privatization.

In the past, AIT's campus in Vietnam relied heavily on fax communications with Bangkok. Staff now use e-mail and the Web extensively to keep in touch with international colleagues and to remain informed about developments outside Vietnam. Students regularly use online resources and this differentiates them from the public education sector in Vietnam. According to one AITCV lecturer, 'It is a big difference between the international education system and the local Vietnamese universities. They are still closed. Students have the means to access the Internet every day.' AIT 'use the net very aggressively and in a lot of the courses they are also given references to the Web sites. They also do project work using data on the net.' However, as in most educational institutions, the Internet has so far had a much greater impact on communications between lecturers than it has on teaching.

Educational Technology and Student-Centred Learning

Many educational commentators in Britain, North America and Australia see the use of technology as leading to a more student-centred learning environment. For example, the British Council's advice to students contemplating distance education courses highlights the ways in which the medium puts new demands on learners. The new electronic technologies used in distance learning can provide students with far greater involvement in the process of learning. These interactive technologies also allow students the exercise of far greater control over that process than is possible in many traditional learning environments. This means that students must take more responsibility for, and be more active in, their learning - whether that means attendance at a satellite downlink site, participation in a class listserv, or delving deeper into a WWW-based lesson. This sense of responsibility is thought to enhance the learning experience.

Of course, there are many different ways of using educational technologies and it is not necessarily the case that educational technologies 'allow students the exercise of far greater control', as the British Council puts it. Whether this is the result is a matter of design, and it is just as easy for lecturers to use educational technology in ways that rigidly circumscribe students' options. In some cases, replacing structured face-to-face teaching with computer-based learning has allowed students to choose when and how they study. This often requires students to be more self-motivated and develop the confidence necessary to be able to work more autonomously. In South East Asia, educational commentators are increasingly promoting the use of educational technology as a way of enhancing the creativity and inventiveness of students. In Singapore and Malaysia, these personal qualities are seen as essential to future national economic development. An article on the role of IT in shaping the education of the future published recently in Malaysia's Star newspaper expresses this sentiment well: The education of this and next century must build a knowledge-based society where individuals are expected to be more creative, innovative and productive.

The workplace of tomorrow will require employees with multiple skills, who are able to think creatively, to solve problems in novel situations. It will not be enough for universities to provide individuals with knowledge, important though that knowledge is. They must provide individuals with the skills to communicate, to venture, to lead. Individuals who succeed in the marketplace-and in life-are generally those with the ability and talent to solve problems creatively and effectively. The Singaporean government believes that educational technology will, in itself, encourage such qualities. Singapore's Prime Minister Goh Chok Tong has states that, 'We will use IT to encourage students to learn more independently, to learn actively.' From the highest levels of government there is an explicit strategy of encouraging students 'to engage in more active and independent learning'.

This policy has begun to have an effect on tertiary education in recent years, with Singapore's leading universities stating that they will encourage creativity and thinking skills in the curriculum and move away from a heavy reliance on written examinations as the sole form of assessment.

Interacting online

It is important to bear in mind the cultural nature of these skills. A student's ability to engage in technologically-mediated communication requires an understanding of the cultural conventions of the medium. People have to learn how to use the telephone-how to talk to an unseen other, how to adopt a 'telephone' voice appropriate to the type of conversation being engaged in and how to gauge meanings in the absence of visual cues. Likewise, e-mail correspondence has a different etiquette to letter writing and synchronous chat discussions operate differently to face-to-face group discussions. In all societies, students may find communicating online just as intimidating as in person. One lecturer with considerable experience teaching mixed groups comprising Australian and South East Asia students in both face-to-face and online discussion forums had come to the conclusion that South East Asian students 'were much more active if they felt secure in the online environment and they would talk in ways they would never do in class.' He has kept online discussion groups small and closed for that reason, thinking that if he opened the discussions up to more participants and outsiders, the South East Asian students would feel more vulnerable. When teaching online courses to students located in both Australia and Singapore, he found that the Singaporeans preferred to e-mail him directly rather than posting public messages, which could be read by other students. He would often either direct them to post publicly or post their response publicly with their consent.

The Cultural Politics of Global Educational Media

The new media made possible by technological advances are agents of cultural pluralism. The dominance of mass media leads to cultural homogeneity, whereas the narrowcasting made possible by Internet-based publishing tends towards cultural diversity. Multimedia is used as an agent of cultural pluralism, within local cultures and across global diasporas and group affiliations', thereby allowing for 'dispersed sites of cultural representation that might serve as a counterbalance to the forces of cultural centralisation'. They emphasise the possibilities afforded by the technology, acknowledging that cultural centralisation is also possible, given the nature and ownership structures of the new media. The ease of publishing on the Internet makes it possible for consumers of information to become producers, effectively democratising media production. However, in practice, the most popular Web sites are those that are affiliated with large media organisations that can afford to produce regularly updated high quality content. While there are perhaps more 'little players' than there have ever been, leading to a diversity in online content production, the number of 'big players' reduces with each merger.

4

Resource Requirements in Education

The planning for EFA should be integrated into wider education sector, poverty reduction and development frameworks to ensure that EFA receives the attention and the priority that it requires, as well as the budgetary allocations that are needed if national EFA goals are to be secured. The demands and the needs of those who are excluded from educational opportunities must be met. Finally, it argues strongly that civil society should be closely engaged in the formulation, implementation and monitoring of strategies designed to achieve EFA. These challenges are neither new nor straightforward but must be addressed if EFA is to become a reality. The extent to which there is a comprehensive approach to planning for EFA is also examined. The weight that is given to the achievement of EFA goals in Poverty Reduction Strategy Papers (PRSPs) is analysed, and a preliminary assessment is provided on the scope and the nature of the engagement of civil society in planning, given its importance as an indicator of national commitment to EFA. The World Education Forum underscored the urgency of developing ways of mitigating the impact of

HIV/AIDS on education and developing education strategies to combat the pandemic. It also recognised that countries in conflict or facing reconstruction require special attention.

Children excluded from school, girls education and the participation of disabled learners were among the issues discussed. Community partnerships in education and the role of non-governmental organisations, school health and nutrition, literacy and education, early childhood care and development and the application of new technologies for education also received attention. Internationally, there is an enormous fund of knowledge and comparative experience on how to provide good quality education for young children, how to promote gender equality, and how to reach the poor and the excluded. This knowledge is not always shared or well communicated but it exists. The realisation of Education For All requires sustained political support, realistic choices about the allocation of scarce resources, and an environment that enables people to engage in an inclusive process of making plans and taking decisions. It is also about developing a global understanding of EFA that underpins support for international investment in education.

EFA National Action Plans

The National EFA Plans by 2002 at the latest is interpreted as meaning any new plan should encompass all of the Dakar goals and result from a strong and politically credible process, then the target has been met in only relatively small group of countries. A completed plan is not necessarily one that has been adopted by

Government and approved as the basis for budgetary allocations in the mainstream of sector and development policy. In some countries, the plans are a restatement or reformulation of existing plans. And the extent is to which there engagement with civil society that goes beyond set-piece consultation has not always been well defined. If a broader and wider interpretation of planning for EFA is used, where in countries are revisiting their goals and targets for EFA, building on existing sector strategies and plans, and promoting EFA in other planning processes such as PRSPs, then there is a much stronger case to be made for a larger group of countries. One preliminary conclusion that can be drawn, illustrated by the twenty-two countries presented in Table 1, is that the Dakar planning commitment is perceived primarily as an exercise for developing countries. There are some exceptions to this, however, as the creation of sub-regional forums for the Nordic and Baltic countries and for three Caucasus states demonstrates. Spain is developing an EFA plan and there is similar work underway in Eastern European countries such as Estonia and Republic of Moldov.

Table 1. National EFA plans, completed or expected to be finalized by the end of 2002

Arab States	Djibouti, Mauritania
Asia	Bangladesh, Cambodia, India, Kazakhstan, Kyrgyzstan, Nepal
Latin Americ /Caribbean	Cuba, Dominican Republic, Ecuador
Sub-Saharan Afric	Angola, Cameroon, Central African Republic, Chad, Ethiopia, Guinea, Guinea-Bissau, Namibia, Niger, Senegal and Zimbabwe.

However, it is broadly true that industrialised countries do not see the goals of EFA as providing the parameters for national education planning. Indeed, this perception is not restricted to planning and can be applied to EFA in more general terms. This has important implications for EFA as a global commitment. Based on a questionnaire survey carried out in June 2002, UNESCO headquarters has collected data on EFA-related planning activities in fifty-four countries. These data suggest that 70 per cent of the countries have set up EFA Forums. They also suggest that 75 per cent of the sample countries are engaged in planning processes that encompass some or all of the Dakar goals, whether in the form of a separate and distinct National EFA Plan or within broader planning frameworks such as education sector plans and national development strategies. The survey records some of the difficulties that confront education sector planners: the lack of reliable data, inadequate technical skills for policy formulation and planning, the absence of robust analyses on costs and the financing of EFA, and the associated difficulty of developing reliable budget projections. UNESCO's Regional Bureaux have conducted their own surveys of planning for EFA. These provide headline information on the status of plan development, difficulties that are being experienced and the existence of related planning documents and frameworks. From this information it is possible to draw some additional but tentative conclusions. Five EFA regions are examined briefly below.

In the nineteen Arab States, all but one country is recorded as having set up a national EFA team or committee. Five countries (Iraq, Libyan Arab Jamahiriya, Palestinian Autonomous Territories, Syrian Arab Republic and Tunisia) have prepared the first draft of an

EFA plan. Mauritania having finalised its plan. In East Asia, most of the twelve countries in the region have indicated that their national objectives will derive from existing policy documents and education sector plans and that additional objectives will be defined for EFA components not covered under existing policy documents and plans. Malaysia has already addressed the EFA goals within its existing national education sector development plans. Cambodia is a country that has chosen to develop an EFA plan that encompasses goals and strategies already embedded in existing plans. China and the Democratic People's Republic of Korea are prepared the first version of an EFA Plan.

Of the nine countries of South and West Asia, Bangladesh and Pakistan have developed draft plans. Pakistan has prepared a national EFA Plan for the period 2000–2015. In the draft EFA Plan, it is estimated that the Government can fund 40 per cent of an enlarged budget but that external funding will be required to fill the financing gap. The EFA Plan makes specific reference to the Dakar commitment that no countries seriously committed to Education for All will be thwarted in their achievement by a lack of resources. India's Plan of Action will be finalised by the end of 2002. It will reflect and complement the SarvShiksa Abhiyan programme for Universal Elementary Education (UEE) that is designed to ensure that all children aged 6 to 14 will receive eight years of quality education by 2010, as well as India's 10th Five-year Plan 2002–2007, which includes literacy strategies as well as UEE.

Both Bangladesh and Nepal are scheduled to have finalised EFA planning documents by the end of 2002. In the Latin America and the Caribbean region there are forty-one countries. Here too, existing policies and plans are being revised to take more comprehensive approach to EFA. For example, the Government of Brazil has worked to ensure that the Dakar goals are addressed in its national education plan for 2001–2010. In Bolivia, the existing 20-year plan for basic education and the country's PRSP provide the main frameworks for addressing the goals of EFA. Nicaragua's National Education Plan 2001–2015 indicates that all the goals and strategies of the Framework for Action are included within its structure, an operational framework for 2002–2008 already having been finalised. In Cuba, it is expected that an EFA Plan will be completed in 2002 to complement the existing 15-year national plan of action. In the Caribbean, all countries existing policies and plans that address EFA goals.

There are many more than the twenty-two countries listed in Table 1 working on existing policies and plans to embrace some or all of the EFA goals agreed in Jomtien and under The Dakar Framework for Action. The International Strategy to put the Dakar Framework for Action on Education for All into Operation states that by March 2002, around seventy countries had developed plans for Education for All, although the evidence base for this assertion is not provided. Clearly there is currently so mere thinking and modification taking place regarding education plans and strategies tailored to reflect the strengths of existing policies and plans as well as the relevance of the EFA goals to national circumstance. For example, the government of Democratic People's Republic of Korea is focusing on life skills and the quality of education in the belief that it has met the other goals. There is evidence too of the establishment of EFA Forums and committees even if a new and/or formal EFA plan is not being constructed, although data on the roles, composition and work of these forums are not readily available. For the future, if there is to be an effective monitoring process at the regional and international level, there is a clear need for comprehensive database on country-level legislation, policies and plans. This is a matter that UNESCO, its specialised institutes, and other international organisations should address.

A rapid survey of readily accessible national policy and planning documents developed over the last five years was undertaken for forty countries, the results are indicative, not comprehensive. There were fivebroad objectives are given below:

— Establish whether there has been recent legislative change to strengthen the right to education and provide a strong basis for EFA planning and programme development;

— Identify the primary policy and planning instruments and frameworks for EFA;

— Clear timeliness for the achievement of EFA goals and targets are in place;

— There are commitments to increase or reallocate budgets for EFA; and

— The engagement of civil society in planning for EFA is a reality.

They were selected in order to include a relatively large sample of countries each of which possesses one or more of the following characteristics: low levels of primary school net enrolment, substantial numbers of school age children out of school, low levels of adult literacy, high recent or current prevalence rates of HIV/AIDS among adults, and the incidence of conflict. Countries with large and small total populations were included. Together, these countries comprise 40 per cent of the global school-age population in 1999–2000. The twenty-three countries from sub-Saharan Africa account for 73 per cent of the subcontinent's school-age population while the six countries from South and West Asia account for 94 per cent.

Only four countries in the sample have adult literacy levels of over 80 per cent. Fourteen countries have HIV prevalence rates of over 5 per cent. At least twelve of the sample countries are living with conflict or emergency. Work was commissioned on the extent to which EFA and MDG goals are reflected in Poverty Reduction Strategy Papers (PRSPs), in both the process of their development and their product. Work by Action Aid is also instructive in this regard.

Most significant is legislation for introducing or strengthening the provision of free and compulsory primary education. This is true of Cambodia, Lao People's Democratic Republic, Thailand, Argentina, Guinea, Madagascar, Niger, Nigeria and Uganda. Since Dakar, India has passed its 93rd Constitutional Amendment Bill, which states that education for children in the age group 6–14 years is fundamental right. Legislation is currently being prepared to delineate responsibilities between the central government, state governments and local bodies, define the parameters of anacceptable quality of education and institute mechanisms for redress when the right is violated. In Nigeria, a bill to Provide Compulsory, Free Universal Basic Education is designed to underpin and strengthen Nigeria's Universal Basic Education Programme.

Amendments to Nepal's Education Act (2002) have clarified the concept of free primary education and the role of communities in education. These enactments set an essential basis for strengthening the right to education and creating a platform on which EFA planning can build, placing sound policies in legal framework.

Education for All goals and objectives appear across a range of national, state and province level policies and plans. They appear in overall development frameworks including Poverty Reduction Strategy Papers (PRSPs), with in education sector, subsector and EFA plans, across the strategies of different ministries, and in separate plans and programmes to meet the needs of particular groups of people. The experience of India demonstrates some of these complexities and relationships. Eighteen or 50 per cent have education sector plans that provide the basis for implementing strategies to achieve EFA goals. All but four of the eighteen had sector plans in place prior to Dakar. A further twelve countries have elaborated detailed subsector plans and programmes either within or outside of a wider sector framework. These may reflect particular levels of education such as early childhood care and development or primary education, specific goals or themes such as literacy, or particular groups such as girls, HIV/AIDS orphans or nomads.

For example, in Yemen there is national strategy for literacy, a strategy for girls education and a population plan of action that includes education. Some countries are in the process of developing an overarching poverty strategy, a long-term education sector investment framework and an EFA plan, all at the same time. The pressures to develop these three different levels of policy analysis and planning are often external. They flow directly from requirements established by The World Bank, bilateral agencies working on sector programmes, and indirectly from the wish to respond to, the international commitments made in Dakar and elsewhere. Articulating a productive relationship between the three is challenging, particularly in systems with limited planning capacity. Where countries are developing separate EFA plans, it is clearly important that they are doing so not just to meet an international commitment but in order to respond to national EFA challenges in a manner which strengthens existing planning processes.

Towards the end of 2002, it is extremely difficult to judge the extent to which new and separate EFA plans will have a well-defined place in the pantheon of national planning instruments. PRSPs are taking on increasing importance for overall national development policy and planning in the world's poorest countries. Globally, forty-eight countries are in the process of developing interim or full PRSPs. These are designed to describe a country's economic and social policies over a 3-year or longer time horizon and to be the operational vehicle for translating a poverty Reduction strategy into an action plan an action plan underpinned by sector strategies.

Given the growing dominance of PRSPs, and of their objective of achieving the MDGs, it follows that education and the attainment of the EFA goals should hold a prominent place in their development and implementation. For interim and full PRSPs in twenty-five countries, Action Aid notes that most strategies identify universal primary education (UPE) as key goal and define it invariably in terms of gross enrolment rates (rather than net enrolment rates or completion rates, which are less ambiguous indicators of progress).

Only four countries, The Gambia, Guinea-Bissau, Malawi and Viet Nam, adopt part or all of the gender-related education Millennium Development Goal. Improving levels of adult literacy appears as a goal in ten PRSPs and as key policy action in Ghana, Guyana, Malawi, Mozambique, Rwanda, Uganda and Zambia. Non-formal education features strongly in the PRSPs of Ethiopia and Guinea. Only Rwanda states its intention to operationalise its policies through an EFA Action Plan. Action Aid finds that there is a strong focus on the quantitative aspects of UPE and a heavy emphasis on inputs. It also finds clear evidence of World Bank policy prescriptions including decentralisation, the role of the private sector post-primary education, targeted public subsidies and an emphasis on cost-efficiency.

Most of the PRSPs present a mix of access, completion, quality and financial indicators and in some cases disaggregate these by gender, income, and urban and rural dimensions. Mozambiqueillu states a clear effort to disaggregate data in this way. Most countries refer to the Millennium Development Goals (MDGs) relating to education and/or to the EFA goals in the education strategies within the PRSPs, but they do not necessarily use the EFA goals as the basis for selecting key education outcomes. The sixteen countries on the level of convergence between key education outcomes and MDGs and EFA goals. Universal Primary Education is clearly delineated in fifteen of the sixteen PRSPs, but only seven countries have retained the EFA goal and the MDG for eliminating gender disparities in primary and secondary education.

In most cases, education goals are set out in very general terms rather than as specific outcomes that can be assessed or measured. The eighteen core EFA indicators that provided the basis for the 2000 EFA Assessment are not widely used and most PRSPs do not have clear timelines to match proposed key education outcomes. PRSPs map policy actions in key sectors such as education in different ways, usually at subsector level, but in some cases against broad objectives or themes. There is an enormous array of proposed policy actions, which revolve primarily around increased coverage, improved financing, better governance and management, better quality, increased literacy and improvement in higher education. It is extremely difficult to assess the financial feasibility of education strategies in PRSPs, which in most cases set out a broad global sector or social sector budget. Burkina Fasois unusual in providing detailed costing of its policy actions for education for the first four years of the programme. Three broad conclusions emerge from these surveys. Whether in PRSPs, or EFA sector plans, there is often a failure to develop a clear relationship between the diagnosis of education and poverty on the one hand, and the education outcomes and actions that are proposed in the plans and strategies on the other.

EFA goals and targets

In addition to broad unqualified statements about achieving UPE, all but four of the countries have set specific targets, including intermediate targets. Thus, Mali, intends to achieve 75 per cent primary gross enrolment rates by 2008. Rwanda will increase primary school net enrolment rates from 73 per cent in 2001 to 80 per cent in 2005, to 90 per cent in 2010. Burkina Faso plans to increase the proportion of Grade 1 pupils who will reach the last year of the primary cycle from 60 per cent to 75 per cent by 2010. While in Pakistan, it is fore cost that the participation rate of 5–to 9–year-olds should grow from 66 per cent in 2000 to 79 per cent in 2005 to 90 per cent in 2010. A characteristic of these targets is that they predictquite substantial percentage increases over relatively short periods of time. Eritrea projects an annual increase of 10 per cent in primary enrolment rates, Benin plans an increase of 15 per cent points, from 55 per cent to 70 per cent, in the rate of pupils finishing primary school by 2004–05.

The assumptions that underpin these projections are rarely provided. Targets for the elimination of gender disparities are expressed almost entirely in terms of enrolment, with the occasional reference to time-bound targets for increasing the numbers of female teachers, for example, in Ethiopia and Guinea-Bissau. Cambodia, Guinea, United Republic of Tanzania and Yemen have 2005 targets for lessening gender disparities but there is little direct reference to the MDG fore liminating gender disparities or to the gender-related EFA goal. Targets for adult literacy are set primarily in terms of overall literacy rates. There is rarely reference to female literacy although Mali is an exception.

The target annual rates of growth are usually much more modest than those set for primary education. Assessing goals for the achievement of ECCE and for increasing learning opportunities for youth and adults is more difficult. The evaluation of strategies to improve all aspects of educational quality is also far from straight forward. However, in broad terms the survey of national planning documents confirms the pattern of goal coverage set out in the analysis of PRSPs. Even though targets may be set, the extent to which they determine strategy content is less clear. A better indicatoı of a government's commitment to EFA is the proportion of the education budget allocated to primary education.

Civil society and planning for EFA

The importance of civil society to the achievement of EFA: Learners, teachers, parents, communities, non-governmental organizations and other bodies representing civil society must be granted new and expanded political and social scope, at all levels of society, in order to engage governments in dialogue, decision-making and innovation around the goals for basic education. Governments need to engage with a much broader constellation of people in shaping policy and planning. Creating and sustaining new learning opportunities is dependent upon individual citizens, civil society and non-governmental organizations having a strong role in their design. While governments have the primary responsibility for ensuring that people's right to education is honoured, civil society organisations need to be accepted as policy partners.

While there is a broad body of evidence on the service provider role of NGOs, the evidence is much more limited as regards the engagement of civil society in policy dialogue and planning. However, important work is underway by international and regional coalitions and networks such as CCNGO, ASPBEA and the Global March for the Elimination of Child Labour in charting progress and identifying innovative and productive ways of working, as well as the barriers to genuine participation. Evidence for changes in relationships between government and civil society actors is difficult to assess from official documents. So, the results from the survey of plans conducted by the Global Monitoring Report are supplemented by reference to both the work of funding agencies and the research literature. Participatory planning is a political, institutional and social process. Two issues should be kept in mind.

— It is important to know where the entry points are for an individual citizen to become involved in the process of setting of education priorities. Constitutional and legal rights to education represent an important indicator of what may be possible for civil society engagement.

— There are ways in which's paces to participate are available or have been created. These may be the traditional spaces afforded by governments and the less formal, more autonomous spaces created outside of government.

In some countries, broader governance and development reforms have established new policy processes in which civil society can participate. Much has been written about the influence that decentralisation has had in participatory processes. One analysis highlights a pragmatic approach whereby decentralisation is a policy tool, an approach that relies on organisations and intermediaries that operate between the state and local communities.

In other words decentralisation is a technical and administrative process. Whereas, a political approach to decentralisation has a much broader meaning. It has the potential to open up new channels for participation in the political system and offers new avenues for direct participation. It is to both approaches that The Dakar Framework for Action refers, but the spirit and intention of EFA is directed towards the latter. There is a range of examples of opportunities provided by government to enable formal consultation to take place. In Mali, the decentralization process in the education sector has included wide consultation and dialogue at community level. This has provided opportunities to clarify roles and responsibilities.

In The Gambia, regional consultations on the outcomes of the EFA 2000 assessment and the World Education Forum have taken place. Key documents have been translated into local languages. Consultations have been held across the country including meetings with young people. The Cambodian Government has created a broad-based National EFA Committee that involves NGOs on a consultative basis. Less common are examples at least from the evidence of government documents where more autonomous dialogue and engagement of civil society is an integral element of educational planning in regular and sustainable way.

In Ghana, a national coalition of NGOs and civil society groups campaigns for basic education of good quality for Ghanaian children, irrespective of gender, ethnicity and geographical location. The campaign acts as a pressure group on the government, urging the Ministry of Education and the Ghana Education Service to keep their promise for education reform, free and compulsory universal basic education and Education for All. It is involved in policy dialogue at the national level and carries out research and advocacy activities.

In Bhutan, community participation encompasses not only the building and maintenance of school facilities (especially in rural areas), but extends to the development of non-formal education programmes built around community-learning centres. School head-teachers and elders from the community are responsible for the planning and management of the literacy programmes. There are possibilities for government to incorporate this type of autonomous space activity in a formal and sustainable process of decentralisation. The evidence so far available suggests that the Dakar challenge has been met with a mixed response and that the technical approach is more prevalent than the political.

The extent to which these different forms of dialogue are connected in the processes of policy development and planning is difficult to track. For civil society engagement to expand, strong sense of what constitutes a good planning process is needed. In addition, more spaces are needed to allow review as a matter of course, rather than as part of the occasional consultation. Furthermore, in many countries, international partner agencies are increasingly seeking to provide development assistance through central and sector budget support where domestic policies are judged to reflect a credible national consensus resulting the engagement of civil society.

In some cases, EFA planning appears to run the risk of duplicating or running parallel with existing planning processes. It is important to ensure that systems with scarce technical capacity do not follow this path. It is also necessary for EFA to be argued strongly and energetically across national planning processes. The case for EFA is a strong one, but EFA must not create a fence around itself.

It is a national priority that cuts across many dimensions of social and economic development. The most visible demographic impact of the HIV/AIDS epidemic is the growth in the number of orphans.

In the Democratic Republic of the Congo it is estimated that nearly 1 million children (aged 0 -14) are AIDS orphans. In Uganda, the figure is 810,000 and in Zambia, it is well over half a million. Based on a study of 34 countries (26 in Africa), one estimate suggests that by 2010 there will be 44 million orphans. Of these, 70 per cent of those who have lost their mother or both parents will be orphans of the impact of HIV/AIDS. A global estimate predicts that the number of orphans will continue to rise for at least the next decade. Today's prevalence rates will largely determine the geography of orphans for the next ten years

Planning for HIV/AIDS

The extent to which schools and other education institutions are able to continue functioning as part of the essential infrastructure of societies and communities will influence how well societies eventually recover from the epidemic. The scale of the HIV/AIDS pandemic is set out in stark terms in the on the Global HIV/AIDS Epidemic 40 million adults and children live with HIV/AIDS, 28.5 million in sub-Saharan Africa.

Some 14 million children up to and including the age of 14 have lost one or both of their parents; 508 thousand children died from AIDS in 2001. It follows then that for countries where the impact of HIV/AIDS is high, there are major challenges in planning for, and sustaining progress towards, the attainment of EFA goals.

This is more than 50 per cent of the global total. While the numbers say something about the scale of the pandemic, they cannot convey the real story of being an orphan and the poverty of the life which young children are forced to live. So, in systems that in many cases already require radical sector reforms and significantly increased levels of resources for education, the challenge of planning to achieve EFA is complicated and compounded by HIV/AIDS. The HIV/AIDS pandemic impacts on learning opportunities and education systems in a myriad of ways. Enrolments fall. Orphans become children out-of-school. The gender gap widens. Schools are unable to function effectively so the quality of learning deteriorates.

Resources are diverted from education to meet the demands being placed on the health and welfare services. Ministries and institutions lose skilled and experienced staff that are difficult and sometimes impossible to replace. The impact on teachers deserves particular attention. The World Bank refers to recent research that suggests that teachers are affected in the same proportion as adults in general, sickness evolves over ten years and, on average, during that period, teachers are absent for 260 days. However some evidence emerging from Southern Africa suggests that mortality rates among teachers may be lower than that of the general adult population and that within the profession, rates vary according to gender, qualifications, marital status and location.

An understanding of the complex relationships between HIV/AIDS and Education has developed quite rapidly in the last few years but that the number of detailed local and country studies on HIV/AIDS and education still remains small. For nearly two decades, the response of the education sector to HIV/AIDS has been muted and fragmented. Now, there is a clearer understanding that for a growing number of countries, HIV/AIDS is not just an additional factor that needs to be accommodated in educational planning and practice. It is now a fact of life that requires that every policy, procedure and activity should be reworked and rethought within an AIDS-centred policy framework. This in turn requires major shift in the mind set and the process of educational planning.

Nine policy development and planning imperatives: mainstream HIV/AIDS across the education sector; keep the education system functioning; adopt prevention, care and support as basic principles to guide system and institution interventions and programmes; keep the curriculum under constant review to ensure that it is relevant in a world with HIV/AIDS; ensure that the needs of the poorest and those in difficult circumstances are met; address the gender inequalities that fuel HIV/AIDS; build capacity for the management and control of the epidemic; promote community participation and support; and work multi-sectorally and with a wide range of partners.

Strategic planning which integrates all relevant government structures is needed to protect and sustain systems and to develop measures for achieving EFA within the framework of AIDS. Two years after Dakar there are good examples of efforts that are being made to plan for education in the context of HIV/AIDS, although the 40-country survey does not suggest that planning for EFA within a national AIDS framework is a reality in most countries with high prevalence rates. But Botswana,

Thailand and Uganda provide examples of countries that are taking the task seriously. Botswana has one of the highest HIV/AIDS prevalence rates in the world.

HIV/AIDS has been declared a national crisis, resulting in the creation of a National Aids Coordinating Agency (NACA). This is the secretariat for the National AIDS Council that is chaired by the President of Botswana. NACA is charged with responsibility for mobilising and coordinating a multi-sectoral approach to HIV/AIDS. One result of this approach is that full education sector review has been instituted, backed by research and assisted by external agencies. One study has assessed the impact of HIV/AIDS on primary and secondary schooling and its summary findings are set out in Box 3.9. These findings have policy implications for sex and health education in the curriculum, school and community welfare services, and teacher support and management. In Thailand the situation is different. There has been research on HIV/AIDS stretching over nearly twenty years. After experiencing escalating infection rates in the 1980s, Thailand initiated a comprehensive prevention programme. This included the 100% condom programme targeted at brothels; broad-based awareness activities, which involved many sectors of society ;and strong human rights protection measures. By the end of the 1990s, the number of new infections had fallen by 80% from the levels prevalent prior to the national prevention programme.

Adult prevalence rates are now below 2% although 670,000 adults and children continue to live with HIV/AIDS and there are 290,000 orphans. So while prevalence rates have fallen there remains concern for localized epidemics and children and young adults. Interventions are needed to strengthen and, where necessary, re-orient education and training programmes. This requires strong partnerships across government ministries, NGOs, community organizations, and the business sector, to ensure good programme coverage and a sufficiency of resources to reduce risks among the young.

Schools provide a strong base for teaching sex education but significant education challenges remain, which are being assessed and planned for by a number of ministries. The Department of Health is promoting wider public acceptance of sex education as a necessary part of life. Together with the Department of Mental Health, guidelines are being prepared for a sex-education curriculum across the formal education system.

These include human development, sexual health, sexual behaviour, personal skills, and social, cultural and gender issues. This framework enables the Ministry of Education to develop the detailed school curriculum. Additionally, government agencies and NGOs that provide counselling services are encouraged to network and coordinate their work, share their knowledge and experiences and strengthen the referral system. Box 3.10 provides an interesting example of a response by Buddhist monks.

HIV/AIDS was first recognized in Uganda in 1982. By 1993, the country had the highest prevalence rates in the world. Now, it is one of very few countries to have succeeded in reversing the epidemic. President Museveni announced recently that prevalence rates were down to 6.1% from 30% in 1990, with the most noticeable decline being in the 15–29 age group. The Uganda AIDS Commission was established in 1992 under the Office of the President to coordinate national strategies. Its work has been characterized by a multi-sectoral approach involving a wide range of stakeholders backed by open political commitment at the highest level of the Government. HIV/AIDS programmes are integrated within the country's revised Poverty Eradication Action Plan and HIV/AIDS has a special vote in the national budget.

Under the national poverty reduction strategy, civil society is engaged in the development of the Education Sector Investment Plan (ESIP) that together with support for the networks of People Living with HIV/AIDS has promoted a strong coalition of involvement with HIV prevention programmes. New alliances and coalitions, often with NGOs at their centre, have opened up opportunities for people living with HIV/AIDS to influence policy debate and reduce discrimination and stigma. There is now a public voice able to influence policy frameworks and legal systems in order to eliminate practices that discriminate against those living with HIV/AIDS.

Within the context of Uganda's National Strategic Framework and Action Plan for HIV/AIDS and its own sector planning, the Ministry of Education and Sports has set out nine major objectives for combating HIV/AIDS over a five year period: develop and implement effective policies for the sector; intensify advocacy efforts for children's rights and needs in the context of AIDS; incorporate HIV/AIDS into the curriculum, across all education institutions and non-formal venues; promote skills-based teacher training in colleges; promote AIDS education, counselling and health services support at educational institutions at all levels; foster the welfare of AIDS orphans; build partnerships with community and non-governmental organizations, and undertake joint activities and encourage research on various aspects of HIV/AIDS and its impact on education and related sectors; and promote joint planning, coordination, monitoring and evaluation of HIV/AIDS activities in the education sector.

These broad objectives have been translated into a set of quantifiable goals. For example, by 2005–06, at least 90 per cent of teacher-training collectives will have introduced skills-based modules on HIV/AIDS into their programmes. By the same year, at least 50 per cent of educational institutions will have introduced welfare and support schemes for HIV/AIDS orphans, 80 per cent of the institutions will have started HIV/AIDS counselling and health services, and at least five major research studies on education and HIV/AIDS will be underway.

The action plan utilises a wide variety of communication strategies. These include workshops, training kits and modules, competitions for best article or performance, the use of radio, video and television, lobbying and out reach activities, T-shirts and trophies, curriculum redesign, press campaigns, national debates, parental involvement and joint projects with community organizations. These three countries demonstrate the value and importance of education policies and plans for HIV/AIDS that are clearly part of a wider and well-integrated national effort that is designed to create and build close relationships across groups, communities, associations and faiths. This national effort has to deal with the impact of the disease on key national institutions including strategies for personnel and human resource support, retraining and replacement. It needs good research and the means to use and communicate the findings. It is also critical that strategies are gender sensitive. There is a growing international resource, on which those charged with policy development and planning responsibilities can draw: the newly established UNAIDS Inter-Agency Task Team on Education.

A new World Bank strategy document concludes that providing a basic education to children and especially equal opportunity for girls, is among the most promising directions in responding to HIV/AIDS. Long-term strategic planning, school-based prevention programmes, peer education and focus on youth, support for orphans and out of school youth, multimedia campaigns and strong partnerships, national and international, are all seen as essential.

Universal Primary Education (UPE) in developing countries have been completed during the past two or three years by groups of researchers at UNESCO, UNICEF and the World Bank. Their main purposes are to estimate the affordability of UPE and the extent to which external aid may be needed to supplement domestic resources.

The costs of achieving UPE by a given date are determined by combining the pattern of enrolment growth over the intervening years with the resources allocated per student over the same period. Most studies focus upon public expenditures and consider whether present expenditures per student should be maintained, or adjusted over the longer run.

The simplest approach has been to assume no change, whereby the cost estimation exercise is reduced to projecting the flow of pupil numbers over time, multiplied by their present unit cost. However, if school quality is judged to be too low, allowances to increase unit expenditures are usually made.

Additionally, if school systems are very inefficient, the possibility of introducing reforms to reduce unit costs may be explored. Sometimes these adjustments are made by directly changing the assumed level of future unit costs.

Alternatively, a more formal modelling framework can be used in order to simulate the cost impact of policy change. The UNESCO and UNICEF studies provide examples of the former approach, whereas the World Bank study is an example of the latter.

Coverage of the developing countries in the three studies was rather different. Although the UNESCO and UNICEF studies demonstrated similar coverage of the developing world, the former also included all of Eastern Europe and Central Asian countries, the majority of which are classified as developed. The 63 lowest-income countries with populations of over one million, home to 75 per cent of all children out of school globally.

However, the actual simulation exercise covered only 47 countries, over two-thirds of which are in sub-Saharan Africa. Another 49 countries, judged at risk of failing to attain UPE by 2015, were not included.

Sixteen of these are eligible for low-cost International Development Association (IDA), loans and have populations of less than one million; 33 are richer countries eligible for normal World Bank loans, including Chile the Islamic Republic of Iran, Malaysia, Mexico, Thailand and others.

Table 1
EFA cost studies: number of developing and transitional countries covered

Region	*UNESCO*	*UNICEF*	*World Bank*
East Asia/Pacific	20	20	2
Eastern Europe/Central Asia	27	9	4
Latin America/Caribbean	29	27	3
Middle East/North Africa	16	18	1
South Asia	9	8	4
Sub-Saharan Africa	50	46	33
Total	151	128	47

Achievement of UPE

The main assumptions and methods used by the studies are summarized in Table 2, and some important points of difference are worth noting. The UNESCO and UNICEF studies each adopted the achievement of net enrolment ratios (NERs) of 100 per cent by 2015 as the criterion for the successful implementation of UPE. The World Bank study adopted completion rates of 100 per cent as the criterion for success.

The completion rate is defined as the total number of pupils who successfully complete the final grade of primary school, expressed as a percentage of the total population of children of school-leaving age. EFA efforts have focused heavily on getting children enrolled in school, rather than on completion rates or student learning outcomes. Data on the number of children completing primary education are often not known. The World Bank estimates the number of pupils completing the final grade of primary school by deducting the number of repeaters in this grade.

Since this does not take into account final-year dropouts, the authors accept that their estimates are an overstatement of the true primary completion rate. Completion rates are important indicators of successful implementation of EFA. For that reason, they are alluded to in the wording of the UPE goal.

Length of the primary-school cycle: The enrolment projections presented by each study are, without exception, based on the current duration of the primary-school cycle in each country. However, the World Bank, uses a standard six-year period to calculate resource requirements. This is done in order to avoid biasing estimates of the external financing requirements towards countries with longer primary cycles and away from countries with short ones. Their cost estimates are therefore biased downwards because primary education cycles exceed six years in over one quarter of developing countries.

The World Bank study made the most concerted effort to collect accurate and up-to-date enrolment, expenditure and funding data. In particular, it utilised the global network of World Bank personnel to provide data for countries that are poorly covered by the UNESCO annual statistical surveys. The other studies relied on UNESCO data, which are compiled from questionnaires completed by Ministries of Education in each Member State. Information about recurrent and capital expenditure on primary education by governments, donors, households, non-government organizations and other stakeholders is poor in most developing countries. What schools actually receive from government is invariably markedly less than what is indicated in official estimates of expenditure and other

Table 2.

Key parameters and assumptions used in the three UPE cost studies

Parameters and assumptions	*UNESCO cost study*	*UNICEF cost study*	*WORLD BANK cost study*
General			
Criterion for UPE	100% NER	100%NER	100%completion rate
Number of countries studied	151	128	47
Target date	2015	2015	2015
Length of primary span	Actual	Actual	6 years
Current unit costs (US$,2000)	188.2	42.4	32.0
Unit costs with policy measures (US$,2000)	198.0	140.8	79.0
Projections			
Using present unit costs	yes	yes	no
Using adjusted unit costs (with reforms)	yes	yes	yes
Assumptions for private enrolments	–	–	10%
Assumptions for economic growth	–	–	not specified
HIV/AIDS included	partly	partly	yes
Capital expenditures included	yes	yes	yes
Target parameters			
Quality reforms			
Pupil-teacher ratio	10% improvement	40	40

Percentage of non-salary costs in recurrent expenditures	–	15%	33%
Efficiency reforms			
Teacher salaries	70%of 1997 levels	–3.5 times	GDP per capita
Repetition	–	–	10%
Financing reforms			
Public revenues as percentage of GDP	–	–	14 –18%
Education expenditures as percentage of revenues	–	–	20%
Primary expenditures as percentage of total education expenditures	–	–	50%

types of income and expenditure documentation. Unit-cost estimates are usually based upon the government's direct funding of the primary education subsector, and do not therefore include the often sizeable expenditures on administration and other key support services (including pre-and in-service teacher training, inspection and curriculum development).

Accordingly, the use of official statistics may often lead to the underestimation of public expenditures per pupil. The data, too, are patchy. For example, in the case of the UNICEF study, information on either unit costs or NERs was missing for more than one quarter of the 128 countries included. In response, the cost estimates in the study were based upon those in countries with similar income or regional characteristics, while NER estimates were based upon known gross enrolment ratios (GERs) and other data. High margins of error in the estimates for individual countries are a likely consequence of these circumstances.

There are important differences in the projection methods used in these studies.The UNESCO and UNICEF studies both provide simple projections of the costs of UPE based upon multiplying present public expenditures per pupil by the projected school-age population in 2015 for each country. However, all three of the studies also provide projections incorporating the impact of policy reforms that are expected to improve the quality and efficiency of school systems. To assume that present public expenditures per student will remain unchanged in the future is unnecessarily restrictive, and the assumptions made about policy reforms can considerably affect the usefulness of cost studies, because the existing pattern of expenditures is usually not optimal. In a large number of countries that achieve UPE, there are still patent needs to improve the quality of schooling, which will usually require increased resources per student. On the other hand, where inefficiencies are widespread, qualitative reforms may facilitate reductions that are badly needed for pedagogic reasons in repetition and drop-out rates, and which may allow costs per pupil, or per completer, to fall.

Accordingly, the diagnosis of the particular resource problems faced by national systems, and of the reforms which could be introduced to tackle them, are important both for the adequacy of the cost estimates and to the encouragement of a process of national reform. Table 2 summarizes the policy measures simulated in each of the studies. The UNESCO study assumed that, in each country, the number of pupils per teacher would fall by 10% by 2015 raising unit costs but that teachers salaries would fall in real terms to 70 per cent of their 1997 levels, thus reducing them. The UNICEF study also assumed a reduction in the pupil-teacher ratio in this case to 40 in countries where higher ratios were found.

In addition, at least 15 per cent of recurrent expenditure being allocated to materials and other non-wage inputs to schooling. Although most of these assumptions make sense, the idea that teachers salaries need to fall in all countries does not: in some, pay will have to rise significantly beyond present levels in order to encourage teacher morale and increase productivity. The World Bank, adopted a more empirical approach. Its policy simulations are based upon the specific premise that education systems in low-income countries that have either achieved 100 per cent primary completion or are relatively close have some basic common features. The study investigates the financing characteristics of 51 countries that have provided the necessary data, distinguishing ten high performing countries from the rest. The authors found that these high performance countries:

- devote a higher share of national resources to public primary education;
- exhibit approximately average unit costs (spending the equivalent of 12% of per capita GDP per public primary student, compared with 13% in the full sample);
- have teacher pay levels which are similar to other groups (spending 3.6 times per capita GDP per teacher);
- spend slightly more of their recurrent budget on non-salary items than other country groups;
- have pupil-teacher ratios of about 40:1;
- and have much lower repetition rates than any of the other groups (8.2% compared with a sample average of 17%). Using these results from the high performance countries as a guide, the World Bank adopted the set of target parameters shown in Table 2 as performance norms for its national simulations.

The other main cost parameters that have been treated differently in the three studies include capital expenditures, private schooling, and the adjustments, if any, made for the prevalence of HIV/AIDS. As regards capital expenditures, the UNESCO study has assumed that the ratio of capital to current spending will remain the same as in the base year. The UNICEF study argues that in most of the 73 developing countries with GERs over 100 per cent, enough school places exist for achieving universal coverage of primary education.

The additional capital expenditure requirements for these countries are zero. This assumption requires that the move to net ratios of 100 per cent can be entirely accommodated by declines in GER, which ignores the fact that many pupils who are currently out of school live in areas where there are no school facilities at all. The UNICEF study also overlooks the impact of population growth: in many countries, the increment to the school-age population over a fifteen-year period will exceed 50 per cent, which is substantially greater than the present gap between gross and net ratios. In such cases, even if GERs and NERs were equalised at 100 per cent (and ignoring the problem of school location), the present number of school places would still prove to be inadequate by 2015. For the remaining 55 countries, it has been assumed that 15 per cent of total education expenditure is being spent on capital investment. Furthermore, in the absence of adequate data, it also assumed that the proportion of total education outlays allocated to primary schooling is about the same as for recurrent expenditure.

The countries where no capital expenditure data were available have not been specified. None of these studies consider the possible impact of teachers working double shifts or of multi-grade teaching on capital spending. Yet these policy options can have a major impact not only upon the number of teachers needed (and thus upon the pupil-teacher ratio), but also upon the number of classrooms required during the move towards UPE. Since these studies aim to provide estimates of the public cost of attaining UPE, the extent to which people choose to educate their children in private schools needs to be considered, because its incidence may reduce the amount of public spending required. The World Bank study the only one to do so assumes that 10 per cent of a given age group will be enrolled in private schools, based on the observed average in the sample of countries for which data were available.

Since this is the sample mean, for many countries it will prove to be a strong underestimate of private provision. Furthermore, it could be argued that the trend towards private schooling may well accelerate as development proceeds. Finally, the World Bank study was the only one of the three to adjust its estimates to allow for the particular costs of the HIV/AIDS pandemic in the countries covered. The three main areas of potential impact are: lower enrolment growth rates, increased teacher morbidity and mortality, and increased numbers of orphans and of other children directly affected by the epidemic. United Nations population projections utilised by all three studies have been adjusted to take into account the demographic effects of the epidemic. Accordingly, even though great uncertainties remain about the impact of the epidemic on fertility levels, each of the studies allows for the impact of the disease on the primary-school-aged population. In addition, the World Bank study attempts to assess the impact of the epidemic on teachers and orphans.

The mortality rates for teachers will be similar to that of other adults, and that since teachers will be replaced at the new lower salary levels envisaged by the authors, increased mortality will actually tend to reduce teacher costs in future years. Consequently, the World Bank, concludes that the main cost burden of the HIV/AIDS epidemic with respect to the UPE target will be the additional financial support required for orphans. The estimate that US$50 per year (in constant 2000 price terms) will be needed to maintain each maternal and two-parent orphan in school. The combined impact of these two assumptions on the total costs of achieving UPE is significant. The annual costs of UPE to a government are a product of the required enrolments by the target date and public expenditures per student at that time. Total costs are determined by how these two factors change over the intervening years. It should by now be clear that the process of estimating these apparently simple magnitudes is in fact rather complex.

A significant body of assumptions is needed, each of which is capable of influencing projected outcomes. Obviously, estimates which use different assumptions cannot be expected to generate exactly the same results. However, it is reasonable to expect that they would not entirely conflict. Indeed, the process of compiling separate estimates which differ in detail, but which suggest the same type of conclusion, is an important means of providing evidence and support for desirable policy change.

Additional public expenditures required the results from the three studies can be compared mainly by examining their conclusions concerning the extent to which public spending on primary schooling will need to increase in order to achieve UPE. For 46 of the countries included in the World Bank study, estimates of the average additional public expenditure required annually over the period to 2015 implied in each study. These estimates have been made using different unit cost figures and the base-year figures differ substantially, with the average across all countries being much higher in the UNESCO study than the others (Table 2).

Further variation occurs because of the different mix of quality and efficiency reforms used for of each study to estimate future unit costs, so some significant degree of variance in projected outcomes is to be expected. It is not possible, from the data provided in the documents, to compare projected expenditures with and without reforms at national level and thus to enable the separate impact of the assumptions made in each study to be identified. The estimates suggest that public spending, in all the countries taken together, would need to increase, on average, by between $4.3 billion and $8.4 billion per year over the period.

The UNICEF and UNESCO studies both produce closely similar results for these aggregate figures, while the World Bank estimate is some 70%–95% higher than the other two. However, it can be seen from the table that many of the estimates for individual countries differ by a much larger margin. The difference between the maximum and minimum estimates is often very wide, with more than a three-fold difference occurring in 24 (52%) of the country cases. Although the UNESCO study uses higher average unit cost estimates than the others, the World Bank study estimates the highest additional costs in 32 of the countries, while the other 2 generate the highest estimates in 7 countries each. If the highest and lowest estimates are summed for each country, it can be seen from the last three columns of the table that the range of average annual additional costs increases from a minimum of $3.2 billion to a maximum of $9.4 billion over the years to 2015.

External funding requirements

The World Bank, is the only one of the three to provide

estimates for the extent of external funding required. This figure is derived by comparing the expected public resources available for primary education spending (derived according to the assumptions shown in Table 2) with the pattern of expenditures required to achieve UPE. The resulting annual gaps are summed and then averaged over the 15-year period. They project that the external funding requirement for primary education will peak at US$4.5 billion per annum in 2015.Sub-Saharan Africa will require 85% of this external assistance. Five countries have annual external funding gaps of more than US$100 million per annum (Democratic Republic of the Congo, Ethiopia, Nigeria, Pakistan and the Sudan), which between them account for nearly 42% of the total external funding requirement. Another seven countries are projected to require, on average, US$50 100 million per annum in donor support. Aid requirements appear to be surprisingly small for countries such as Bangladesh, Malawi, Mozambique and Zambia, especially in view of current levels of donor support to their education sectors. India is projected to have a sizeable surplus of domestic funding for primary education, averaging nearly US$1.4 billion between 2000 and 2015.

Much could be said about the pros and cons of the values adopted for the target parameters in the World Bank study. However, they are broadly similar to those suggested by some earlier work, and in other ways they are consistent both with known research results and with common sense. For example, many poor countries with high cost systems are unlikely to be able to universalise provision unless something is done to reduce unit costs. In several francophone African countries, high teacher costs are compensated by very high pupil-teacher ratios, and total costs are met by reducing enrolments relative to other countries at similar levels of income. Thus the salary bill is affordable, but it brings negative consequences for both the quantity and quality of provision. As in other areas of public policy, there are clear choices to be made that are capable of affecting the possibility of services being universalised.

Nevertheless, while it may be unproblematic to advocate moving the parameters in the directions indicated by the more successful country cases, it should be recognized that the actual mechanics of doing this will often be very difficult indeed. As the World Bank, acknowledges, teachers salaries provide a good example. Where these are very high relative to GDP per capita—as in Eritrea, Ethiopia, Haiti, Lesotho, Niger, Central African Republic, Rwanda, Mozambique, Zimbabwe and others 8 it often reflects structural characteristics of the economy (such as a general shortage of skilled people, or a highly agrarian economy with a small formal sector), the effects of which cannot easily be disregarded. In such economies, the salary ratios not just of teachers, but of all professional workers tend to be higher relative to per capita income than they are in more industrialized countries, because the level of teachers salaries is a product of the remuneration demanded by skilled and professional workers as a group, and cannot necessarily be affected in isolation.

More generally, teacher salary level is also a function of the structure of the economy, which cannot easily be altered as a matter of short-or medium-term policy choice. One response, suggested by the World Bank, is to recruit a new cadre of teachers at lower salary levels, while continuing to pay existing staff on the old scales. A number of countries, including Senegal and

Mali, have adopted this approach with some success. However, the impact on average salary levels is slow, and it remains to be seen whether such a double salary level for teachers can become the dominant mode of employment for the profession as a whole. A second example is provided by average rates of repetition, where the target rate, in the World Bank, is set at 10 per cent for countries currently above this level, with no change envisaged for other countries. There is no doubt that high rates of repetition are dysfunctional. They are symptomatic of a discontinuity between the demands of the curriculum on the one hand, and the ability of schools and teachers to impart it, on the other.

Improvements in the quality of schooling and curriculum reform provide two ways in which high rates of repetition can be tackled. In some countries, however, policies of automatic promotion have been introduced often in the absence of reforms to improve childrens learning. In these circumstances, observed repetition rates can be a poor efficiency measure. Where progression to the next grade is virtually automatic, as in many of the high performing countries identified in the World Bank study, the learning outcomes of children may actually be lower than in those having end-of-year examinations which determine the possibility of progression within schools. Although repetition rates may be lower in the former group, they may be an inadequate proxy for learning outcomes. This is not to argue that repetition rates should not be reduced, but rather that the ways in which some of the high performing countries have achieved these reductions may not necessarily provide the best model for policy.

The assumptions for revenue and public spending appear to be defensible in principle, but very ambitious in practice, and one way of assessing just how ambitious is to consider their implications for the extent of real expenditure growth on primary schooling over the projection period. The World Bank's simulations suggest that total expenditure on primary education in the 47 countries would need to have risen from $7.4 billion in 2000 to $23.3 billion in 2015 an expenditure growth of 8% per year in real terms over the 15 years. By the final year the gap between domestic financing and total expenditures is expected to amount to $4.5 billion. This implies that domestic resources available for expenditure on primary schooling would, in 2015, amount to $18.8 billion in these countries. In order to assess the implications for the required growth in domestic financial resources, we need to know the extent of external financing of primary schooling in these countries in 2000. This is not precisely known, but an amount of $1 billion would be consistent with the aid estimates and roughly consistent with an average funding gap of $2.5 billion over the 15 years, in the Bank study. In this case, the required growth of domestic resources, from $6.4 billion (i.e.$7.4 billion domestic expenditure, minus aid resources) to $18.8 billion, would amount to a growth rate of 7.5% per year over the 15 years. If domestic resource availability were less than this in the base year, its subsequent required rate of growth to 2015 would be greater than these estimates suggest.

These increased domestic resources have to be generated by economic growth, on the one hand, and/or by fiscal reform on the other. However, the recent growth record of the economies in these countries is not promising (33 of the 47 countries are in sub-Saharan Africa, where, during the 1990s, weighted real GDP growth was scarcely more than 3% per year). If this growth record were not improved, shifts in sectoral expenditure, together with more fundamental fiscal reform, would need to provide the remaining 4.5% annual real growth in resources. These expenditure shifts would represent major increases in resource requirements, and it is by no means clear that such strong and sustained changes will take place.

The gap between domestic resources and required expenditures could increase sharply. For example, if the 47 countries were able to increase real domestic resources for primary schooling by 5% per year over the 15-year period (which would be a substantial achievement), the resource gap in 2015 would amount to $9.9 billion rather than the $4.5 billion projected in the World Bank study. Furthermore, under these circumstances, the average gap to be filled by aid would rise from $2.5 billion to $4.2 billion per year over the fifteen years. All attempts to assess the costs of achieving UPE must be carried out on a country-by-country basis. Estimating likely resource requirement estimates at the regional or world levels underestimates global needs for three main reasons.

— All estimates are extremely sensitive to the values of unit costs and these can be properly addressed only at the country level.

— For cost purposes, enrolment projections conducted at world or regional levels are misleading since those countries having reductions in pupil numbers because of declining school-age populations are implicitly added to the enrolment increases required elsewhere.

— The financing gaps in countries unlikely to be able to finance UPE themselves should not be added to surpluses elsewhere.

Thus, aggregated methods of counting either enrolments or costs will not produce helpful results. For this reason, we have included only those recent estimates that have been based upon country-level analysis. It has been shown, however, that these estimates differ substantially from each other. The differences illustrate the sensitivity of the cost estimates to the data used in the analysis, to the assumptions used about the extent of required or desirable policy change, and to the assumptions made about future rates of economic growth. As regards costs, there is an urgent need to improve the quality of information on public expenditures on education. There appears to have been a deterioration in the quality of these data in recent years, and without some sharp increase in coverage and quality all attempts to estimate resource requirements will be undermined. Partly as a result of this quality decrease, there are substantial differences in the unit cost information adopted in different studies, and this is one of the more important causes of their varying results. The results provided by the World Bank are the most comprehensive and dependable.

Methodologically, they are superior to those in most other recent work, and the simulation framework employed allows most of the key policy variables to be integrated with the analysis. However, the World Bank almost certainly underestimates both the expenditure implications of the move to UPE and the external aid requirements quite considerably.

— It covers only the countries furthest away from UPE, with populations over one million. Up to one quarter of children at present out of school live in countries not covered by the Bank's analysis.

— Its adoption of a six-year primary cycle for all countries ignores the additional costs of UPE in 25% of countries with longer systems.

Both of these factors imply that the costs of reaching UPE are underestimated. The estimates made for the size of financial gaps are also reduced by the same factors. Although many of the countries omitted from the analysis should not encounter great difficulty in financing their move to UPE, some of them will undoubtedly need sustained external support.

In addition, however, it is likely that the assumptions concerning the speed of policy change and the extent of required fiscal reform envisaged in the World Bank study are too demanding. On reasonable, but still ambitious, assumptions for revenue growth and fiscal reform, it seems likely that the size of external aid requirements in the 47 countries will be up to two-thirds higher than those projected in the study. If the speed of implementing the proposed quality and efficiency reforms were to be delayed, the discrepancy would be even greater.

Finally, there are some categories of policy change and resource provision that have not been covered adequately by any of these studies. These categories are of considerable importance to EFA and to a number of the goals, including those covering formal schooling. They include the treatment of gender, the impact of HIV/AIDS and the situation of countries in circumstances of emergency.

Gender Targets and the Demand for Schooling

Each of the studies assessing the costs of UPE accepts

that strong supply-side, expansionary policies to support increased enrolments will be needed over the coming decade, but they do not attempt to analyse the costs of increasing the demand for schooling. Their emphasis is upon measures to improve and increase the number of schools, classes, teachers and materials. They also accept, albeit with more cursory treatment, the importance of measures to improve the quality of schooling, since low quality undermines both the value of schooling and the willingness of parents to enrol their children. Is there demand for girls and boys schooling? It has become clear, however, in recent years, that supply-side policies though critically important will be insufficient to achieve schooling for all.

Research has shown that a central explanation for the continued under-enrolment of children from poorer households lies in the direct and indirect costs incurred when these families send their children to school. Such costs include, but are by no means limited to, the fees charged by some schools and countries as a condition for school attendance. Governments increasingly find that fees are not helpful to enrolment growth at primary level, and that they directly undermine the goal of achieving UPE. Even in 'fee-free 'systems, however, there are many other direct costs of attendance. These include the costs of uniforms (or better clothes for children than would otherwise be needed), books, sports fees, voluntary school contributions, transport and the like.

These costs are often high, both absolutely and relative to public expenditures on schooling. For example, in six African least developed countries (LDCs) for which there are data (Ethiopia, Guinea, Malawi, Uganda, United Republic of Tanzania and Zambia), private household expenditures per pupil during the 1990s were, on average, slightly less than half the level of public recurrent expenditures per pupil. In addition and often of even greater significance for poor households are the indirect costs of income foregone arising from the reduced availability of child labour when children go to school. These opportunity costs are strongly felt even if the children themselves do not directly generate cash income, because they often substitute for adult household labour thereby releasing older household members for remunerative work.

The distribution of these direct and opportunity costs is unequal by gender and by household poverty. For example, the loss of girls labour is, in many African non-pastoral households, more keenly felt than that of boys. Equally, the direct costs of school attendance are often greater for girls owing to higher costs for their clothing, and for greater security for them while travelling to school. Expected future benefits to households also differ by gender. Many parents expect that the education of their sons will eventually bring them greater benefits than what they could expect from educating their daughters. All such cost and income differences are perceived more acutely, the lower the income of the households concerned. For these reasons, measures are required to reduce the private costs of educating children if UPE is to be achieved. Such cost-reduction measures are most strongly required in the case of children and particularly girls from the poorest households.

Some types of cost-reduction can best be achieved by macro changes in policy. School fees can be abolished. Charges for books, sports and other items can also be removed. It can be argued that these types of cost-reduction policy are more efficient than compensation schemes, provided that differential cost-incidence for richer and poorer households is not an explicit aim of policy. In any case, charging differential fees to rich and poor households is not usually possible, owing to the practical difficulties of means-testing at the school level (although South Africa is an exception). The magnitude of other elements of direct costs, such as the costs of clothing and transport, cannot be easily affected by governments or other service providers. The indirect costs are even more difficult to compensate by such means. Thus, for the very poorest households with numerous children, school enrolment in many countries will probably remain patchy. As countries develop and become richer (provided that distributional policy facilitates income growth for the poor), indirect schooling costs will become smaller relative to household incomes, and enrolments among the poorer segments of the population will, accordingly, rise. But these enrolment benefits of income growth, delivered by the development process, may take a good many years to materialize.

Educating children in extreme poverty situations

Furthermore, and more worrisome for the achievement of the international development targets, income growth that is dependent upon market processes alone risks excluding those in extreme poverty, because poor people do not participate in these processes. These groups, having neither significant incomes nor assets, find themselves ineligible for credit. For them, all available household labour may thus be needed in order merely to subsist. Thus, even where schooling is fee-free, the costs of sending children to school for these households are relatively greater than the costs for households that are relatively better off. Furthermore, such costs may be absolutely greater for the poorest households because they have to rely on child labour to a greater extent than the others. As mentioned, the existing cost studies make no estimates for these kinds of demand-side adjustments. Although the World Bank, explicitly states that its projections are based upon primary schooling being free, and although a set of policy options are mentioned which recognize the need to target the education of girls, these adjustments have not been integrated into the cost-estimation exercise. To what extent might this omission understate necessary costs? Clearly, there is no easy answer to this question since the extent of private costs from school fees, other direct costs and opportunity costs varies significantly across countries, and there are no consistent data to assess their magnitude.

Where school fees still exist, their removal implies increased costs to the state for each and every child, in a typical range of 5%-15%. Furthermore, as has been shown above, the African data suggest that the removal of both direct and indirect costs to the poor may require an increased cost to the public sector of up to 50% of current public expenditure per student for the families involved. If this is an upper bound to the extent of subsidy needed, the costs follow directly from the proportion of poor households eligible for the benefits of the scheme. For example, if the government decided to provide a subsidy equivalent to 25% of existing public spending per pupil to the poorest 10% of children in areas where attendance rates were very low, this would increase unit costs across the system by around 2.5%. Arguably this would count as a fairly modest increased cost if it were instrumental in shifting net enrolments from 90% to a level closer to 100%.

The main instrument available to reduce the weight of private costs (once fees and other charges have been removed) is some form of targeted income-supplementation scheme (ideally progressive, and related to the poverty of the household), conditional upon school attendance. This could be designed either in the form of scholarships, or of income transfers linked to attendance and performance of designated children in school. Such schemes are likely to be needed to provide a short-cut to achieving UPE, by accelerating the enrolment changes that may eventually be delivered by the process of economic growth. There are two additional reasons for using income supplements.

— They provide not only the means for directly securing enrolment growth among the poorest families, but also an additional way to achieve the poverty-alleviation targets required by the Millennium Development Goals. By facilitating a change in time allocation, away from child labour and towards schooling, they reallocate the incomes of the poor towards investment in human capital. This is crucial to securing not only short-run school attendance targets, but also longer-run income growth for poor households.

— Facilitating more continuous school attendance among poorer children, income transfers can be instrumental in reducing rates of repetition at primary level. Evidence from schemes in Latin America, such as Bolsa Escola in Brazil, suggests that the impact of income transfers on school efficiency can be substantial. Where this is so, savings in the average cost of primary school completion for poor households can substantially reduce the net public costs of an income-transfer scheme.

The implication is that such schemes could be partly self-financing through their impact in reducing repetition rates, and thus provide a useful additional means to support a rapid transition to schooling for all. Programmes providing financial incentives for improving enrolments and gender equity in schooling have also been implemented, with donor support, in a number of African countries.

These include the USAID-funded scholarship programme for girls in four pilot schools in Ghana, the GABLE fee-waiver programme for non-repeating primary-and secondary-school girls in Malawi. By 1998, 1,500 girls - representing approximately 1 per cent of total female lower-secondary enrolment had received support. The programme was successful in increasing female secondary-school participation, but less so in improving female school-achievement.

Gender considerations for policy in targeting

Programmes targeting girls are not always popular. Evidence from Malawi indicates that many parents resent girls-only benefit programmes, because boys from poor households are also often unable to attend school. Furthermore, even with fee-waivers, it appears that very few girls from lower-income groups attended secondary school. Since the children from higher-income families were more likely to obtain better primary-school grades than were children from poorer families, more of them continued to secondary school. In these circumstances, incentives would have been better targeted at needy, primary-level children. Careful identification of eligible groups, as happened in the United Republic of Tanzania, would have been an important condition for success. Although targeting is a difficult process, communities can usefully be involved in selecting the beneficiaries, and some of the target groups requiring financial assistance are relatively easy to identify. The base-year costs equal the total government primary education expenditure per pupil for the year of data collection.

The proposed incentive programmes mainly concerned rural girls, and they provided a cost-per-beneficiary in the range of $30 -$100. Strategies to provide incentives for girls were judged to be particularly important in Ethiopia, Ghana, Guinea, Mali and Senegal countries with low enrolments and wide gender gaps. In Ethiopia, where demand for girls education has been particularly low, for example, the proposed subsidies to cover the cost of stationery and exercise books, and of material for school clothes, would represent a substantial incentive for households to send their girls to school. If the subsidy were targeted at rural areas in disadvantaged parts of the country where enrolment is lowest approximately 20 per cent of school-aged children could benefit, thus generating a 9 per cent increase in the base-year unit cost for Ethiopia.

But the potential benefits in terms of girls enrolments are substantial. Proposed subsidy programmes in other countries where demand for girls schooling has been low could be designed so as not to have a major impact upon unit costs. For example, in Ghana, Guinea, Mali and Senegal, increases in unit costs as a consequence of the proposed subsidies for rural girls would range from 0.6% in the case of Senegal, to 5% in Ghana.

In general, then, the additional costs of removing gender inequalities need to be considered as a separate demand-side item which must be added to the mainly supply-side calculations of the costs of attaining UPE. This is particularly necessary for the poorest households in low-income countries. The examples given above are merely illustrative of what may be needed. But they suggest that effective incentive programmes for girls or, more generally, children from poorer households to attend school might add at least 5 per cent to the average unit costs of primary schooling. In the 47 countries included in the World Bank, this would translate into $1.3 billion extra public spending by 2015, in comparison with spending in 2000, adding about $0.4-$0.6 billion to the average annual additional expenditures required. These increased costs would be likely to increase the size of the average funding gap presently projected in the World Bank study by perhaps 20% although this would need to be calculated country-by-country to provide a reliable guide.

The costs to education of HIV/AIDS

It is now seen with greater clarity than ever before that countries where HIV/AIDS prevalence is high are experiencing severe problems in maintaining progress towards the attainment of the EFA goals. This section outlines the risks that HIV/AIDS poses for the attainment of primary schooling for all, and its resultant cost implications. Some attention will also be given to the implications of HIV/AIDS for the attainment of the goals relating to the elimination of gender disparities in schools and improving educational quality, in so far as both of these are closely linked to primary schooling for all.

Finally, some recent initiatives to assess the costs of HIV/AIDS to education sectors will be considered with a view to estimating the additional finances that must be raised globally for the attainment of EFA in an environment where the prevalence of HIV/AIDS is high.

The HIV/AIDS pandemic has implications for both resource (supply) and cost (demand) in the achievement of the EFA goals. Resources are either mobilized domestically or come from external financing. The adverse macro-economic impacts of HIV/AIDS affect domestic resource availability in the public sector, and constrain the flow of resources from the private and household sectors. The epidemic also affects educational provision in ways that may increase or decrease the need for the financial resources that must be provided if the EFA goals are to be met by 2015. Education systems are highly vulnerable to HIV/AIDS.

The fundamental technology of one teacher with a class of ten to a hundred students has remained the same for thousands of years. Educators and education-support personnel constitute the largest proportion of public service employees worldwide. The vast numbers of students to whom they reach out constitute a significant proportion of the population. All told, an education sector may well involve a quarter or more of a country's population. Because it is so person-intensive, the sector is particularly exposed to the way HIV/AIDS can scythe its way through its personnel and operations, affecting the present adult generation in the persons of educators and support personnel, and the coming generation in the persons of learners.

An education system also comprises mainly young people. The majority of learners are in their pre-teens,

teens, or early twenties, while a substantial proportion of educators are in their twenties and thirties. With the partial exclusion of those in their pre-teens, learners fall into the age groups where HIV infections most commonly occur, while educators are in the age groups where AIDS deaths are most frequent. These older age groups also encompass the parents and families of the majority of young learners, implying that for many learners participation in educational programmes occurs within the context of extensive HIV/AIDS sickness and death in their families and communities.

Adapting to these AIDS situations necessitates significant changes in school programmes. It also necessitates adjustments of management and policy frameworks at systemic level. Some of the response strategies have financial and cost implications that can be quantified. Others involve responses that impinge on costs, but in ways that are difficult to quantify. Still others have qualitative dimensions that will not affect costs until such time as specific interventions are made to respond to them. The resource and cost implications of HIV/AIDS for the achievement of the EFA goal of good quality primary schooling for all will be examined, therefore, from the following five perspectives: the impact of HIV/AIDS on resource availability for EFA; HIV/AIDS cost implications for learners; HIV/AIDS cost implications for educators; cost implications of adjusting education programmes to HIV/AIDS; and cost implications of the education management response to HIV/AIDS.

HIV/AIDS impacts on the resources needed for the attainment of the EFA goals in two possible ways: by causing the overall resource envelope to be smaller than it would otherwise have been, and by affecting the allocation of available resources. Models that have examined the impact of HIV/AIDS on national economies generally show that the annual GDP growth rate is lower than it would have been in the absence of AIDS, but they do not show any actual decline in GDP. The lower growth rate means fewer resources than in a no-AIDS scenario for the various categories of public spending, including education. The epidemic could also potentially affect both inter and intrasectoral resource allocations. If the epidemic leads to an increased proportion of public resources for health or other sectors, this could entail a smaller proportion for education. Thus, for some countries, achieving the target set by African leaders at the Abuja Summit in April 2001 to allocate at least 15% of their annual national budgets to their health sectors may limit possibilities for growth in education budgets.

The World Bank has proposed that the financing measures for the attainment of the EFA goal of universal primary education of good quality include an increase in the allocation to education from the current average of 17.5% of national budgets to 20.0%. In high-prevalence HIV countries, other claims on national resources might jeopardize the possibility of securing and maintaining this increase. Intrasectorally, HIV/AIDS is likely to augment the resource needs of other education subsectors. This is because the impacts on educators at these levels are as severe as at the primary school level, but the costs of replacements and training are considerably higher. Because much teacher specialization occurs at post-primary levels, the loss of mathematics or physics teachers, or of third-level lecturers in specialized areas, is difficult and costly to absorb.

The impacts of HIV/AIDS on human resources in society could also generate a need at secondary and tertiary levels to increase numbers, at least in certain areas, to make substantial curriculum modifications, and to introduce new areas of study and practice. AIDS increases the need for, but reduces the supply of, qualified individuals in certain skilled areas. This is very apparent in the health services, where in a climate of increasing demand, AIDS mortality is high. For instance, it is projected that in South Africa the demand for health services could be more than 11% higher in 2010 than in a no-AIDS scenario, whereas experience to date is that almost one-third of the nurses graduating from the University of Natal die within a few years of their graduation.

The premature death of adults in their most productive years depletes the skills base of society and calls for an accelerated production of replacements. But these replacements need to be equipped with current knowledge, understanding and skills, and with the more intangible qualities of resourcefulness and adaptability. This is because the AIDS-loss of qualified personnel makes it necessary for others to move over sideways and take over the responsibilities of departed colleagues. In an AIDS-affected society, graduates from vocational and other third-level programmes need more than their highly compartmentalized professional skills. They must also be flexible, adaptable and innovative in response to the needs of the fast-changing and unpredictable AIDS world. Assessing the impact of AIDS on the skill needs of the labour market, bringing about the necessary curriculum developments, increasing the output of qualified individuals with the necessary qualities, and introducing new programmes of study and skills development; all call for additional resources or for new formulas in allocating existing resources.

The cost implications of responding to them could affect the resources needed to progress towards the EFA goals. Following the past pattern of allocations and concerns, the EFA areas most likely to be at risk would be adult literacy and early childhood care and education. The allocations to these areas tend to be insufficient to mark significant progress towards the agreed targets. They could become even more insufficient because of responses to HIV/AIDS needs at the secondary and tertiary levels.

HIV/AIDS affects the private and industrial sector negatively by reducing productivity, increasing costs, diverting productive resources, and affecting the market for business products. These factors combine to reduce the profitability of private enterprise, leaving it less well resourced to support educational developments. At the individual and household levels, the impacts are immediate and sharp. Many AIDS-affected households, which previously contributed cash and other resources for educational programmes, can no longer do so. The sickness, poverty and hunger that the epidemic has brought in its wake have left many rural communities so weakened that they cannot participate as in the past in self-help community activities for school maintenance and development. Resources, which in a no-AIDS situation would have provided for the development of the infrastructure needed for EFA, are no longer forthcoming.

HIV/AIDS affects the size of the school-age population in three principal ways: fewer births occur because of the high death rates among adults aged 20-40, their biologically most productive years; HIV-infected women have lower fertility rates, and about one-third of the children born to HIV-infected mothers are likely to acquire HIV infection perinatally, with the majority of them dying before they reach school-going age. The combination of these factors results in the population of school-going age being smaller than it would have been in a no-AIDS situation. One recent projection suggests that by 2010, the population of school-going age in Zimbabwe will be almost a quarter smaller than it would have been in a no-AIDS situation, while that in Zambia will be one-fifth smaller (Figure 1).

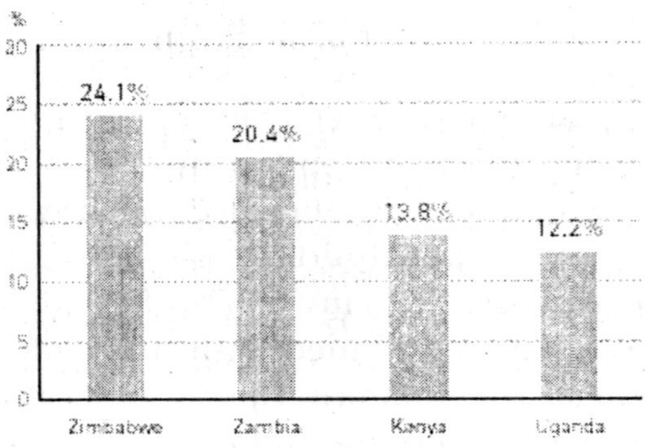

igure 1: Projected reduction (%) in size of primary school-age population, 2000-2010

his implies that the financial burden for attaining universal primary education in high-prevalence HIV countries will be lower than it would otherwise have been. Fewer learners will require fewer teachers, fewer educational materials and fewer classrooms. Projections for Botswana, South Africa and Zimbabwe suggest that HIV/AIDS will lead to actual population decline (and not just to a lower rate of growth) in the coming few years, while demographic projections for Swaziland suggest that the population of primary school students will begin to decline absolutely from 2007. Should this occur, the costs of educational provision would in principle be lower than the current costs. Children affected by HIV/AIDS HIV/AIDS affects school participation for three different groups of children, making it difficult for them to enrol in or complete school, or to attend school on a regular daily basis.

The first group -those who themselves are infected with HIV will not be large. Projections for South Africa are that fewer than 1.2) of school-age children in any calendar year will be HIV-infected and that a much smaller proportion will be carrying the burden of AIDS illnesses. The extent to which such children will enrol in school, or continue once they come to know their HIV status, is not known. The school participation of infected children might imply some additional costs (such as for transport to facilitate their medical supervision). Their families might also need subsidies that would encourage school attendance on the part of the infected children and that would cover some of their medical costs. But given that the percentage of infected children would be small, these costs would also be relatively small.

The two other groups orphans and HIV/AIDS-affected children however, are much larger, and many factors prevent them from attending or completing school. Moreover, the epidemic is increasing the salience of these factors. Chief among them are: Cash costs poor families, in rural areas and urban shanty towns, have always found it difficult to meet the cash costs associated with schooling. HIV/AIDS aggravates this difficulty by leading to losses in production, decline in family incomes, and increased medical costs.

Family and household responsibilities a significant proportion of households, particularly in rural areas, finds it difficult to do without the contribution to the household economy that comes from the labour of children, particularly girls. Because it impacts negatively on the household economy, HIV/AIDS has increased this situation. Orphans carry an additional quota of psychological, social and material difficulties.

The emotional loss they experience at the death of a parent is compounded by the dislocations they subsequently undergo. Within their new surrogate family, orphans are frequently at a disadvantage compared with the biological children.

Micro-studies of small communities show that orphans frequently come last in line when food is being apportioned, carry a disproportionately large share of household chores, and do not participate in school to the same extent as children who are not orphans. They also experience greater health risks than non-orphaned children and are more likely to be stunted and malnourished.

HIV/AIDS has also led to the emergence of child-headed households in which there is no adult and where the children must fend for themselves. Access to school is on a very precarious footing for children in such households. There may be no way of meeting school-related costs, or nobody may be free to go to school because everybody must work to generate the resources needed for survival.

Cost implications

To ensure that the EFA goal of primary schooling for all can be met, it is necessary to ensure that every orphan or child affected by HIV/AIDS can attend school and complete the education cycle. Fees, school-related costs, the salience of their labour in the household and the additional burdens experienced by households that provide orphan care, collectively constitute the principal obstacles to the full participation of these children. The full school participation of orphans and HIV-affected children will thus depend particularly heavily on removing all compulsory cash costs associated with school attendance, and upon the provision of targeted subsidies to mitigate the direct and indirect costs for households with orphans. The cost of any social subsidy scheme depends on two factors: the size of the target group and the amount of the subsidy. This Report takes the position that the subsidy programme should target all orphans (these will normally include those in child-headed households) and all children from poor families that have been affected by HIV/AIDS. There is no strong evidence to suggest that paternal orphans are less disadvantaged educationally than maternal or double orphans. Preferably, therefore, a target group defined by orphan status should extend to all orphans. The case for the inclusion of other vulnerable children is also strong.

— Because of its impacts at the household level, HIV/AIDS is making it more difficult for children from families where there is infection to participate or continue in school.

— Targeting orphans only and excluding other vulnerable children runs the risk of putting orphans into a special class that would accentuate their sense of being different, increase their social and psychological problems and expose them to subtle forms of discrimination.

In its simulations for the costs of attaining the EFA target of universal primary education of good quality, the World Bank (2002 a includes provision for orphan support, but limits this to maternal and double orphans. The Bank's AIDS Campaign Team for Africa (ACTafrica) seems to have adopted the same approach in estimating the costs of scaling up HIV programme activities across Africa, defining orphans as those under 15 who have lost a mother or both parents to AIDS. This is in accordance with the definition given by UNAIDS in 2000, but more recently UNAIDS has defined AIDS orphans as children aged 0 -14 who have lost one or both parents to AIDS. Extending the meaning of AIDS orphans to include all who have lost one or both parents to AIDS would greatly increase the costs for orphans included in the Bank's simulations.

The published costs are global estimates that include costs arising from AIDS-related teacher provision. However, it is relevant to note that orphan estimates for 34 countries in 2010 show that maternal and double orphans are likely to account for approximately 55% of the total number, and paternal orphans for 45%. On this basis, the increased costs of including paternal orphans in the simulation would amount to approximately $100 million per year. In the absence of good data on the number of other vulnerable children who would need assistance, extending the estimates becomes very much more difficult. In sub-Saharan Africa, there were 42 million out-of-school children in 1998, and in South-East Asia 46 million.

At that time, the adult HIV-prevalence rate was 8.0% in sub-Saharan-Africa and 0.7% in South and South-East Asia. It is not unreasonable to assume that 8% of the out-of-school children in Africa belonged to families where there was HIV or AIDS, and 0.7%) of those in South-East Asia. Application of these figures suggests that the number of out-of-school children from HIV/AIDS-affected families could be approximately 4 million. Orphans could, of course, be included in this number.

Although it may be on the low side, the figure provides a starting point for estimating the number of children from AIDS-affected families who would need the incentives of subsidies to promote their school participation. There are considerable differences in the size of subsidy proposed for orphan support. The World Bank applies a fixed rate of US$50 (in 2000 prices) per year per maternal or double orphan to the estimated population of such children in the school-age population. The Bank's earlier ACTafrica document proposes US$9 - $35 as the cost per child for community assistance with living expenses, and US$25 -$33 as the costs per child for school expenses. The latter, however, is a weighted average of primary and secondary school costs based on estimates from the United Republic of Tanzania. Moreover, while the school expenses of orphans and other vulnerable children would represent a cost to an education ministry, this cost arises in the attainment of the EFA target of free primary education and is not, in itself, determined by the HIV/AIDS situation.

There are two channels through which HIV/AIDS leads to the permanent loss of educators to an education system and teachers to classroom work, namely death and withdrawal from the teaching profession. Although some evidence seems to point to increased teacher mortality in the presence of HIV/AIDS, a more guarded view is that the rate of HIV infection among teachers is the same as in the rest of the adult population. But even in this view, the loss of teachers to AIDS may be very considerable. A model for Zambia predicts that, given the HIV prevalence in the adult population, the number of teachers would rise from 37, 000 in 1999 to 50, 000 in 2010, while in a no AIDS scenario the number would have risen to 59, 550. While the absence or death of non-teaching educators can seriously weaken an education system, the death of a teacher in active service brings immediate negative classroom consequences. Sometimes these are irreversible. Unless there is immediate replacement, something that seldom happens in the most severely affected countries, a whole class will be left without a teacher for a considerable length of time. This teacher loss puts at risk the very possibility of offering education to all children.

Absenteeism

For several years after initial infection, most HIV-infected people remain clinically healthy. But eventually the virus destroys so much of the immune system that the infected person becomes susceptible to infections that a non-infected person would normally be able to ward off. This leads to episodes of illness, followed by periods of apparent good health. The periodic bouts of illness usually increase in number and duration over time until they fuse and become almost continuous. Infected teachers are unable to teach when they experience these illnesses. This leads to frequent casual absenteeism on their part, and eventually to their being placed on formal sick leave. Drawing on research at the Imperial College,

London, the World Bank uses the estimate that an infected person is likely to be unable to teach for a total of 260 days prior to death from AIDS. AIDS also leads to considerable absenteeism on the part of healthy teachers. Two factors contribute to this: caring for sick relatives at home, and attending funerals.

Since the burden of care falls mostly on women, female educators and office staff frequently find themselves pulled between the demands of their professional work and attending to sick persons who require almost round-the-clock care. In addition, de rigueur participation in funeral rites for relatives, colleagues and community members leads to teachers being frequently absent from class, sometimes for days on end.

Education systems that are losing teachers, whether through death or early retirement, must make good those losses through the training of additional teachers. Otherwise the education systems will not be able to provide education for all who are in need; moreover, the quality of that education will suffer. Additional training is a cost that is attributable to the impact of HIV/AIDS on teachers themselves and on the workforce in other areas. The replacement costs can be estimated, firstly, from knowing the number of teachers who are likely to leave the system permanently and prematurely because of death or taking up appointments elsewhere, and secondly, from knowing the training costs. Account must also be taken of death benefits, payable on behalf of teachers who die while in service, to which an education system may be contractually obliged. Anecdotal evidence from Malawi and other countries is that meeting these obligations (by providing coffins, transport and cash) is crippling the operations of district education offices which find the outlays for these purposes absorbing the resources that would otherwise have supported school supplies and inspections.

Absenteeism due to AIDS-related sicknesses represents a major loss to education systems. Since no benefits accrue from the salaries paid to educators for the periods of absence, the systems lose the benefits of these resources. If they provide replacement teachers to cover for those who are absent, they will also face additional financial costs and these costs will be attributable to HIV/AIDS. In high-prevalence HIV countries that have not yet attained universal primary education, education systems seldom have the resources to provide replacements. Hence in these countries teacher absenteeism because of HIV/AIDS imposes major declines in quality and efficiency, which will further delay the achievement of the EFA goals.

For several reasons, HIV/AIDS is likely to boost the overall costs for training teachers. Teacher-training institutions (colleges and universities) will suffer AIDS losses among their staff in the same way as schools, but securing replacement staff will be slower and more costly than at school level. An enlarged and possibly accelerated training programme will be needed to make good the number of teachers and teacher trainees lost to AIDS.

There will be need to adapt the training programme to make future teachers appropriately competent to teach understanding of and response to HIV/AIDS. Higher mortality of professionals in other sectors will increase the mobility of surviving teachers, further increasing the unit training costs of those who stay in the schools.

The South African National Conference on HIV/ AIDS and Education in May-June 2002 indicated that while South Africa was currently training about 3, 000 teachers each year, by the end of the decade, without ARV drug intervention, more than 20, 000 would need to be trained. In the same country, more than 30% of nurses have been dying within three years of completing their studies. It may well be the same for teachers, especially women. The implications of these phenomena for teacher training are huge. Yet little thought has been given on how best to address these needs, and even less has been given to the cost implications of satisfactory and feasible responses.

One simulation for Zambia projects that teacher absenteeism due to HIV-related illness will result in the loss of 12, 450 teacher years or close to 20 million teacher hours over the period 1999 -2010. At a pupil-teacher ratio of 40:1, this is the equivalent of 498, 000 children being left without classroom instruction for a year. The absence of a system for the placement of temporary teachers is a problem facing many countries.

More problematic is the fact that a pool of suitably qualified individuals available for temporary appointment does not at present exist. Its creation would imply costs for training and for temporary personal emoluments.

Even though the salary costs of such temporary teachers would be less than for a comparable number of qualified permanent staff, their provision would represent a major additional AIDS-originated cost in ensuring that all children have access to primary education of good quality.

HIV Prevention Education

In a world where HIV/AIDS is so dominant, schools and education programmes have a cardinal responsibility to equip those for whom they have responsibility with the knowledge, skills, attitudes and values that will reduce the likelihood of their acquiring or transmitting HIV infection. This means that education programmes should seek to empower learners to live sexually responsible, healthy lives. The first and basically correct response of education ministries to the HIV/AIDS crisis has been to strive to incorporate aspects of HIV/AIDS, sexual and reproductive health (SRH), and life skills education into the school curriculum. Studies from seventeen countries show the concern of education ministries to integrate these areas into school programmes with a view to the promotion of behaviour change. However, for a variety of reasons, 'the school system has failed to develop a coherent, comprehensive approach to HIV/AIDS and, more generally, SRH education.

The root problems arise from: a curriculum approach that does not acknowledge HIV/AIDS and SRH education as a professional subject area in its own right; curriculum design that tends to spread HIV/AIDS, SRH and life-skills education thinly across a number of carrier subjects and fails to make the all-important links with health education and health services; teaching methodology that places reliance on whole-class teaching in formal settings, and to some extent with examination performance in view, but with little room for peer teaching, the participation of communities, or the involvement of persons living with HIV/AIDS; teachers feeling inadequately prepared to teach this area, and being reluctant to deal with sensitive and, in some cases, taboo topics; and inadequate curriculum and teacher support, with insufficient (if any) accurate and good quality teaching and learning materials, and little provision for systems of back-up guidance, training, teacher support structures, monitoring and evaluation such as other subjects receive. The potential of curriculum changes to empower school learners to avoid HIV infection will remain severely compromised until these issues have been adequately addressed and HIV/AIDS education has been fully professionalized. Such provision cannot be made without incurring costs.

UNAIDS has enumerated some of the variables affecting the costs of school and education HIV/ AIDS programmes. In a somewhat modified and amplified form these include:

— *personnel:* required for consultancies, establishing and maintaining a corps of trainers, providing backup guidance and teacher support structures; programme development: the amount of time and type of work invested in developing HIV/AIDS school curricula and supporting materials; production and distribution of educational materials: the quantity and quality of educational materials produced for each student and teacher covered by the programme;

— *training school teachers*: workshops and other training sessions for school staff; and monitoring and evaluation, conducting impact assessments, and other forms of research. However, anticipate improvements in service delivery and envisages that one-third of total recurrent spending on primary school services will be dedicated to non-teacher salary inputs (administration, support services, textbooks and other pedagogical supplies, along with subsidies to encourage the school attendance of children in difficult circumstances). The proportion is said to be adequate to cover whatever costs may be involved in the provision of HIV/AIDS preventive education. Such an approach, however, could put high HIV-prevalence countries at the disadvantage of being left with a smaller share of their non-salary resources for other quality-enhancing inputs.

ACTafrica examines the costs of HIV/AIDS education programmes for those in schools and for out-of-school children and youth. For education programmes aimed at learners in primary schools, the cost per teacher trained is either US$75, for a simple programme and the provision of basic materials, or $200 per teacher for a more sophisticated programme that includes the development of training materials and the establishment of the school curriculum.

The cost per secondary-school teacher is given as US$121 for a simple programme and US$241 for a more extensive programme. Finally, it is estimated that it would cost US$8.-$11.80 per person reached to provide suitable peer education for out-of-school children and youth (in the age ranges 6 -11 and 12 -15). The overall costs of extending coverage by 2005 so as to reach 60% of the primary-school teachers, 80% of secondary-school teachers, 15% of out-of-school children aged 6 -11 and 50% of those aged 12 -15 are estimated as US$211 - $313 million annually for all of sub-Saharan Africa.

Although substantial, these costs are not sufficient to provide coverage of the entire target groups. Nor do they include provision for the production and distribution of textbooks and teaching materials, for providing the back-up support required, or for developing and establishing an appropriate curriculum at college and university levels for the preparation of college lecturers and professional pre-service training of teachers. If the ACTafrica cost estimates were apportioned equally over primary, secondary and out-of-school youth education, that estimate for primary education would be of the order of US$90 million annually, or an average of more than US$2 million per country. Education ministries might be reluctant to draw this amount -which would be far from sufficient to meet all the needs -from the resources for non-teacher salary inputs.

The trauma so frequently generated by HIV/AIDS has become a major care and support issue within schools. The experience of psychological distress or discrimination causes some young people to discontinue their education or to participate erratically. Others may find that they have more difficulty in learning. Prior to the advent of widespread HIV/AIDS, teachers encountered these problems less frequently. But with AIDS it is different and it is worse. The epidemic makes schools home to increasing numbers of intellectually, socially and psychologically dysfunctional learners.

However, not enough action has been taken, or even planned, for the establishment of the necessary psychological support systems. The work of school guidance personnel pertains more to providing vocational guidance than psychological support. A survey of education ministries in thirteen SADC countries, conducted in 2001, shows awareness of the problem and the inadequacy of the steps being taken to deal with it. Eleven countries stated that they had no programme of social support for infected or affected learners. Twelve also stated that neither teachers affected by AIDS, nor those who are dealing with AIDS-affected children, were being helped to cope. Such support as was available came through ad hoc, under-funded and uncoordinated NGO activities.

The principal variables that have a bearing on the additional costs that HIV/AIDS entails for the achievement of EFA goals are:

1. training additional teachers to replace those dying from AIDS;
2. providing death benefits that education ministries must pay to those who die while still in service;
3. mainstreaming HIV/AIDS within the curriculum, principally through the introduction of HIV preventive education;
4. developing, producing and disseminating textbooks and learning materials for HIV preventive education;
5. mainstreaming HIV/AIDS into programmes for teacher preparation;
6. managing functions and activities for propelling a proactive response from the system;
7. increasing capacity to provide counselling;
8. re-orienting primary education curricula; and providing incentives to stimulate school participation by orphans and other children affected by HIV/AIDS.

Simulations have dealt principally with the first second and final items on the above list. They have also given much attention to the costs that teacher absenteeism represents for education systems. But as already indicated, the absence of teachers on prolonged sick leave or for other AIDS-related reasons, will have incremental cost implications for the achievement of EFA goals only in circumstances where payments are made for temporary teachers to cover for those who are sick or absent. Severely affected countries need to make provisions to do so. Within the context of the achievement of EFA goals, the cost implications of items 3 to 8 in the above list have not been incorporated into any model, and no attempt has been made to estimate their costs at either national or regional levels. This is not because they are not important, but because of difficulties in getting bases for the cost estimates and because there may be some misapprehension that the costs of these soft items may be dwarfed by teacher and orphan costs.

The ACTafrica estimates for the cost of extending the coverage of youth activities, although not cast in an EFA framework, suggest that the curriculum and various school programme costs might well exceed those involved in teacher replacements and may well be comparable with those arising from absenteeism estimates. Ensuring the achievement of EFA goals also necessitates attention to demand factors, especially on the part of children who are in any way disadvantaged by their personal encounter with HIV/AIDS. Orphans stand out clearly as a category that should be supported, with the support extending to all orphans of school-going age. But orphans are not the only children that AIDS puts at a disadvantage in relation to living conditions and schooling. Children from poor families who have experienced AIDS are also in need of incentives that improve their living conditions and encourage their school participation. Thus the cost implications of HIV/AIDS for the attainment of EFA goals arise from four broad areas:

1. incremental teacher costs for the training of additional teachers to replace those lost to AIDS and for the payment of death benefits;
2. the costs of training and paying temporary teachers to supply for those on extended periods of sick leave;
3. incremental school and education programme costs for mainstreaming HIV/AIDS and responses to it into the curricular and other areas of school life; and
4. orphans and vulnerable children costs for social subsidies to encourage or enable the school attendance of children from families affected by AIDS.

The annual spending on these areas should be in the order of US$975 million. This figure is 74 per cent more than the World Bank 2002 a estimated as the additional AIDS-related costs for 33 African countries. The increase is due principally to making allowance for education programme costs and increased coverage of orphans and other vulnerable children. The continued spread of HIV infection, even in countries where prevalence is already very high, is commentary enough on the failure to date of education programmes to make a significant impact. Widespread, almost implacable, denial, extensive discrimination, combined with potentially lethal lack of information, also indicate that education messages are not getting through.It is unlikely that they will do so until education programmes that respond in manifold ways to HIV imperatives are resolutely mainstreamed into school systems. The funding needed for this has not yet been forthcoming. The Dakar Framework for Action called on the international community to implement as a matter of urgency education programmes and actions to combat the HIV/AIDS pandemic.This cannot be done without mobilizing sufficient identifiable resources for establishing and running such programmes. Dakar also underlined the importance of ensuring that children in difficult circumstances have access to and complete primary education of good quality.

HIV/AIDS has placed huge and increasing numbers of children in exceptionally difficult circumstances. Some it has orphaned. Others it has marginalized and placed at high risk of being bypassed by educational provision. The future of these children, who form a very significant proportion of the next generation, will depend heavily on resources becoming available to safeguard their schooling.

HIV/AIDS and schooling

The World Bank 2002 a estimates have properly demonstrated the potential of the AIDS pandemic to add very substantially to the overall costs that individual countries will sustain in achieving the goal of primary schooling for all (along with gender equity and improved education quality). For high-prevalence countries, such as Rwanda, Zambia and Malawi, the Bank projections show that incremental costs due to AIDS will increase the recurrent budgets by more than 45%. The analysis in this chapter indicates that the budgetary impact of AIDS is even more dramatic. But large as this provision may appear, it must be further augmented by the numerous additional hidden costs, already alluded to, that HIV/AIDS entails, and by the cost implications of the pandemic for the attainment of the other EFA goals. Recognizing that the cost implications of HIV/AIDS are this extensive and pervasive may serve, better than anything else, to demonstrate the urgency of protecting the education sector against the ravages of the pandemic and of using its potential to extend a similar protection to society.

The Dakar Framework for Action requires countries to 'meet the needs of education systems affected by conflict, natural calamities and instability. The theme of education in emergencies became important during the 1990s, in connection with the complex humanitarian emergencies in Afghanistan, Bosnia and Herzegovina, Rwanda, Somalia, the Sudan and elsewhere. Such complex emergencies can last for years or even decades, creating a major barrier to the achievement of EFA. For UNESCO, an educational emergency is a situation of crisis created by conflicts or disasters which have destabilized, disorganized or destroyed the education system, and which require an integrated process of crisis and post-crisis support. This emphasis upon the need to extend support beyond the short term -when special measures are needed is consistent with the Dakar approach.

International and national responses to emergency situations can include: education for refugees, in camp schools or national schools; education for internally displaced populations (IDPs), affected by conflict or disasters; education in situations of armed conflict, insecurity and instability; education in areas of large scale repatriation of refugees and IDPs; and reconstruction of regional or national education systems, after conflict or disaster.

During the 1990s complex humanitarian emergencies began to seem commonplace. By 2000, conflicts in Afghanistan, Bosnia and Herzegovina, Burundi, Iraq, Sierra Leone, Somalia and the Sudan, had each left more than 400, 000 people as refugees in other countries. Other places generating similar flows of refugees during the 1990s included Rwanda and Kosovo, while 39 other countries had been the source for over 10, 000 refugees in at least one year. By 2001, there were an estimated 15 million refugees in the world, including about 7 million in populations categorized as assisted by UNHCR, and 3.7 million Palestinian refugees, assisted by UNRWA. Many refugees were from the developing countries of Africa (3.3 million) and Asia (5.8 million).

In 2001, some 500, 000 persons fled from home-country circumstances which were so dangerous that they were recognized by asylum countries as prima facie refugees. No comprehensive data for refugee education exist, but in the year 2000, UNHCR supported the education of some 835, 000 children at primary and 63, 000 young people at secondary level, often through international and national NGOs working in refugee camps and settlements. Most of the countries at the centre of complex humanitarian emergencies also suffered massive internal population displacements, although information on the dimensions of this phenomenon is less readily available. This is partly because there has been less international access to, and assistance for, IDPs.

Many internally displaced persons live in camps or settlements similar to those for refugees, but others live in the homes of, or alongside, normal populations, in ways less conspicuous and more difficult to quantify. The world total of persons internally displaced as a result of conflict and human rights violations in 2001 has been estimated as at least 25 million people (over 13 million in Africa, over 4 million in Asia and over 3 million in Eastern Europe). In some situations, the national education system provides well-organized education for such people, but in many other places as well, the situation is bleak.

Natural disasters: flooding, hurricanes or earthquakes -affect education systems throughout the world. Sometimes there is major damage to the education system, as with the millennium floods in Mozambique. In 1998, Hurricane Mitch destroyed schools in Honduras, leaving over 250, 000 children at primary and 30,000 at secondary level without access to schooling; the Ministry of Education's central offices were damaged and the bulk of the education archives were lost. Conflict, insecurity and instability pose the greatest challenges to education. Educators often make gallant efforts to keep education alive during times of war or civil conflict. Classes are sometimes held in the open air, in homes and basements, or in damaged buildings of various kinds.

The task of reconstruction follows. In 2000, almost 800,000 refugees in twelve major migrations returned to their homelands. Probably similar numbers of internally displaced persons returned to their places of origin. Even populations that had stayed in place throughout conflict or disaster had to work to rebuild their communities and schools. The tasks of reconstruction of education systems after conflict or disaster present major challenges to education planners and managers.

Resource requirements for emergency education

Emergency education a necessary bridge Education in emergencies sits uneasily between humanitarian aid and development assistance. In acute emergencies, the key institutional actors may focus on survival issues, but the refugees or other emergency-affected populations themselves give a top priority to restarting education. There is now growing recognition of education as the fourth pillar of humanitarian response. Governments such as Sweden and Norway have publicly committed themselves to supporting emergency education as a matter of policy, but there are some others for whom this step remains to be taken. Emergency education is important if the lags between ending humanitarian support and the start of funding from development assistance budgets for reconstruction are to be minimized.

Education is needed early in a crisis, for psychosocial and pedagogic reasons and to protect children. It helps to provide a sense of normalcy and hope for the future, and prevents a cohort of children from missing out on education for life. Adequate resourcing is particularly needed because children affected by crisis or conflict: have special needs for good teaching and learning conditions to help them build a sense of achievement and self-esteem; need opportunities for recreation and expressive activities to help meet their psychosocial needs; may not receive the normal level of emotional and developmental support from their families; may not have access to books or other printed materials; may be in schools which have had their teaching-learning resources destroyed, and where the buildings need to be repaired and re-equipped; and may have teachers who are undereducated and untrained, and who require additional support through training and materials to cope with difficult and unfamiliar situations.

Human resources

In some displacement situations, experienced teachers move with their communities and can resume their teaching duties. However, in many crisis-affected communities, teachers are underqualified and untrained. Even trained teachers may have had limited exposure to modern teaching methods. Crisis may give the opportunity for a new approach to teacher training, which can help even inexperienced teachers develop the skills for effective teaching, as well as taking account of the special needs of children exposed to some form of crisis. Far and disruption make it difficult to maintain an atmosphere conducive to learning, and this can take a grievous toll on school morale.

In Palestinian schools, surveys found that many teachers and students had trouble concentrating, particularly if they had witnessed or experienced violence or had family members in prison or hiding. Education programmes that focus on crisis-affected populations need to include a major component of carefully designed training for teachers and head teachers, for adult educators and for youth educators/youth group leaders. Such training is best provided in-service, through vacation and weekend courses, mobile trainers, and training of mentor teachers in the schools or school clusters, while later there can be use of open and distance learning methods.

Crisis and reconstruction often imply that it is difficult for the government to meet the costs of teacher salaries. Donors have often been unwilling to support salary costs, preferring to provide forms of assistance which carry less risk of long-term obligation. Conventional objects of support, such as educational supplies and materials, the repair or construction of schools, or in-service and pre-service teacher training, are needed. However, recurrent support for teacher salaries is often critical to restarting the system.

In high-profile emergencies, donors may be willing to give generous humanitarian support. Such assistance to displaced populations is often channelled through NGOs, which can act quickly. By contrast, assistance to national government agencies, notably for reconstruction, may face problems of absorptive capacity and effective management. The level of resourcing for emergency education programmes is critical for achieving sustainability. For displaced populations, UNHCR suggests that shelter, equipment and materials standards be developed by reference to the general level of well-run government schools in rural areas near the national capital, rather than the dysfunctional low levels often found in neglected rural areas where refugee camps may be located. If a large refugee or displaced population moves into an area with weak education systems, efforts to raise standards in that area, through mobilizing national and international resources, will be required.

The UNICEF 's concepts of child-friendly spaces and child-friendly environments are helpful. Child- friendly spaces in Albania, for Kosovar refugees, and in tent cities in Turkey after the 1999 earthquake, meant grouping together basic services for mothers and children, including basic health services, early childhood care and development, schools, recreational facilities, psychosocial support, youth activities and mother support. Emergency assistance may include imported kits of educational and recreational supplies, although local procurement is preferable and brings benefits to the local economy. Where possible, heavy duty reproduction equipment for education resource centres is commended, permitting the reproduction of materials to meet urgent educational needs. Governments facing reconstruction situations typically confront huge problems. Even the resources to formulate education needs, develop plans and make them known may be lacking.

The Ministry of Education may lack furniture, typewriters, computers or even paper. Thus there is usually no lack of items upon which external resources can be quickly spent. A major concern in post-conflict situations is to avoid replication of educational structures that may have contributed to conflict. It is important that donors contribute to the softer side of reconstruction, namely consensus-building on integrative approaches to education, curriculum and textbook renewal in support of peace building, and investment in both in-service and pre-service teacher training. Life skills education, including education for peace, human rights and citizenship, are important in situations of protracted post-conflict displacement and reconstruction, and have resourcing implications especially for start-up. There appears to be an initial window of opportunity to initiate such changes, perhaps lasting 18 months. The tasks of negotiating curriculum change for schools and teachers, writing and testing new textbooks, and introducing effective systems of teacher training, require commitments of five years or more. Inter-agency cooperation is obviously needed to ensure the best use of available resources for acute emergency situations and reconstruction. However, estimating the likely annual resources required for such purposes is difficult.

Most emergencies are unpredictable and the resources needed depend entirely on their nature, scale and intensity. What is required, furthermore, is open to different interpretations. In Afghanistan, for example, the estimates of the international community were much lower than those of the Ministry of Education. Even so, the $100 million transitional requirements estimated by the international community exceeded both the commitments subsequently made and the annual average requirements for UPE in 2015 of $70 million projected by the World Bank. These estimates, in turn, were dwarfed by the Ministry's stated need for some $875 million over the two years to mid-2004.

It is difficult to draw conclusions more widely. However, recent history would suggest that at least four or five countries are likely to face major complex humanitarian emergencies during the course of the next decade, with many more experiencing disaster, conflict and instability to varying degrees. In all of these countries the costs of achieving the EFA goals would then be greater than at present predicted because infrastructure, supplies and human resources would be diminished. Moreover, the means of meeting these costs will be reduced by declining income flows, by human death and displacement, and by reallocation of potentially available resources from education to other, equally pressing, demands.

If the impact of such events were to increase the additional annual costs of reaching UPE by 25% in four or five countries, between \$0.4 -\$0.5 billion would be added to the average annual costs of UPE across all countries. This would increase the projected total costs by 2% to 3%, but if the affected countries were among those which are expected to face financing gaps, it would represent an increase in the Bank's projected funding requirement of around one-fifth. This would be a minimum impact since the capacity to resource education systems in these countries would have been negatively affected by emergency.

The analysis in this discussions indicates that each of the recent studies of the costs of achieving primary schooling for all by 2015 appears to have understated them in some cases, substantially so. It is clear that the World Bank study is, from a methodological standpoint, the strongest of the three. It has a transparent framework that allows the possibility of supplementary analysis in a helpful way. Its data requirements are not extensive, and the main cost parameters that affect the development of education systems are given a central place in its design and operation.

The two other studies also have strengths -both of them use national-level data and employ a generally cautious and sensible approach to the ways in which education systems can be reformed. However, the data they use, particularly the financial information, appear highly variable, and in some cases, unreliable. The generally higher cost estimates that emerge from the Bank study are, in general terms, to be preferred. Nevertheless, the World Bank analysis oversimplifies the cost side -partly by investigating only six-year systems, irrespective of their actual length, and by omitting a number of countries from the analysis which appear, prima facie, to be likely to have some difficulty in achieving the goals.

In addition, the policy reforms proposed for the education systems in the countries covered by the study which directly influence their expected costs -appear to give less weight to implementation difficulties than they might. This is particularly so as regards teacher salaries where the proposed mechanisms for their reduction, relative to per capita income, would present a very demanding agenda for the highest cost countries. Two other aspects of the study hold critical importance for the projected outcomes. The first concerns the revenue side. This chapter has argued that the revenue assumptions upon which the calculations of financing gaps are based are optimistic.

A government completely committed to reforming its approach to the delivery of primary schooling would probably still have difficulty sustaining the real expenditure targets for primary schooling sought by the Bank over a fifteen-year period. Much depends, however, upon progress with economic growth in the countries concerned, because healthy and sustained income growth would more easily deliver the increased resources sought.

The study is silent about the growth assumptions it employs, so it is not possible to assess this part of its analysis. On balance, however, public resources available to primary schooling in these countries appear likely to grow at a slower rate than assumed in the study. This, together with the omissions on the cost side, suggest that the size of the financing gap, from these sources, is likely to emerge as being substantially larger than projected. There are at least three other major omissions from these cost estimates. The first concerns the demand side. There is a need to increase the incentives for families particularly those in the poorest sections of the community to enrol girls in school.

The analysis suggests that the additional expenditures required might amount to $1.3 billion by 2015 in the countries concerned, which would increase the average annual funding gap by about $0.5 billion over the period. Similarly, the analysis suggests that the estimates for the resource requirements of responding to the HIV/AIDS pandemic were underestimated to the extent of approximately $0.4 billion.

Responding to the educational needs of countries in emergency situations might require additional resources of approximately $0.5 billion on an annual basis for those among the poorest countries falling victim to emergencies. All this implies an annual aid bill of the order of $5.6 billion per year being required to support the move to EFA, within the same kind of framework as that set out by the World Bank. This aggregate estimate for average annual aid requirements to support UPE with gender equality in good quality schools is more than double that given in the Bank document.

Some distance from being able to use the country-level resource requirement projections that are currently available as even a rough guide to aid requirements for securing EFA objectives. The national simulations should become the starting point for more country-level work, integrating new national planning effort and data to produce revised outcomes. All financing gap estimates are relatively small residuals that are sharply responsive to changes in the assumptions used to determine the size of the much larger aggregates of national expenditures and resources available. This implies that single-valued estimates need to be replaced by a range showing the extent to which conclusions change if the parameters turn out to be different.

5

Tools of Electronically Developed Education

World Wide Web opens new ways of learning for many people. Now, educational programs and learning materials installed and supported in one place can be used by thousands of students from all over the world. However, most of the existing educational WWW applications use the simplest solutions and are much more limited than existing 'on-site' educational systems and tools. For many designers, an ideal format of educational WWW material seems to be a static electronic copy of a regular textbook: chapter by chapter, page by page, picture by picture. Such electronic textbooks are non-adaptive, i.e., students with different abilities, knowledge, and background get the same educational material in the same form. We claim that adaptivity is especially important for educational programs on WWW which are expected to be used by very different classes of users without assistance of a real teacher (who usually can provide adaptivity in a normal classroom). Currently, we can name very few adaptive educational applications on WWW.

All these applications keep a model of the user between sessions and use it to adapt the teaching sequence and the presentation of the material to a given user. The problem is that adaptive electronic textbooks are 'knowledge-rich' applications and they are not very easy to design. There are some authorinig tools for developing 'static' electronic textbooks on WWW, but there are no tools available to support a designer in creating an adaptive textbook on WWW.

Developing Adaptive Electronic Textbooks

Developing adaptive electronic textbooks on WWW based on the ideas from the areas of Intelligent Tutoring Systems and Adaptive Hypermedia. Adaptive textbooks use knowledge about its domain and about its users. The domain model serves as a basis for structuring the content of an adaptive ET. We distinguish two parts in an adaptive ET: a glossary and a textbook. Both these parts are based on the domain model. The student model is used by an adaptive ET to adapt its behaviour to each particular user.

The key to adaptivity in an adaptive ET are the domain model and the user model. The simplest form of domain model is just a set of domain concepts. By concepts we mean elementary pieces of knowledge for the given domain. Depending on the domain and the application area, concepts can represent bigger or smaller pieces of domain knowledge. A more advanced form of the domain model is a network with nodes corresponding to domain concepts and with links reflecting several kinds of relationships between concepts. This network represents the structure of the domain covered by a hypermedia system. The domain model provides a structure for representation of the user's knowledge of the subject. For each domain model concept, an individual user's knowledge model stores some value which is an estimation of the user knowledge level of this concept. This type of model (which is called an overlay model) is powerful and flexible: it can measure independently the user's knowledge of different topics.

The glossary is the central part of the ET. The glossary is considered as a visualized (and externalized) domain network. Each node of the domain network is represented by a node of the hyperspace, while the links between domain network nodes constitute main paths between hyperspace nodes. The structure of the glossary resembles the pedagogical structure of the domain knowledge and, vise versa, each glossary entry corresponds to one of the domain concepts. The links between domain model concepts constitute navigation paths between glossary entries. Thus, the structure of the manual resembles the pedagogic structure of the domain knowledge. In addition to providing a description of a concept, each glossary entry provides links to all book sections which introduce the concept. It means that the glossary integrates traditional features of an index and a glossary.

A textbook is hierarchically structured into units of different level: chapters, sections, and subsections. To make the textbook 'more intelligent' and to connect it to the glossary, we have to let the system know what each unit of the textbook is about. It is done by indexing of textbook units with domain model concepts. For each unit, a list of concepts related with this unit is provided (we call this list spectrum of the unit). For each involved concept, the spectrum of the unit can represents also the role of the concept in the unit. Currently we support two roles: each concept can be either a outcome concept or a prerequisite concept. A concept is included in the spectrum as a outcome concept if some part of this page presents the piece of knowledge designated by the concept. A concept is included in the spectrum as a prerequisite concept if a user has to know this concept to understand the content of the page. Indexing is a relatively simple but powerful mechanism, because it provides the system with knowledge about the content of its pages: the system knows which concepts are presented on each page and which concepts have to be learned before starting to learn each page. It opens the way for several adaptation techniques presented in the next subsection.

The knowledge about the domain and about the textbook content is used to serve a well-structured hyperspace. The system supports sequential and hierachical links between section. It generates the table of content where all entries are clickable links. In addition, it generates links between the glossary and the textbook. Links are provided from each textbook unit to corresponding glossary pages for each involved concept. On the other hand, from each glossary page describing a concept the system provides links to all textbook units which can be used to learn this concept. These links are not stored in an external format but generated on-the-fly by a special module which takes into account the user's current state of knowledge represented by the user's model. This approach is not only reducing page design time but also provides room for adaptation.

Many more opportunities for browsing the course materials than traditional on-line textbooks. The negative side of it is that there is a higher risk for the user to get lost in this complex hyperspace. To support the user navigating through the course, the system uses adaptive annotation, an adaptive hypermedia technique. Adaptive annotation means that the system uses visual cues (icons, fonts, colors) to show the type and the educational state of each link. Using the user model, the system can distinguish several educational states for each page of material: the content of the page can be known to the user, ready to be learned, or not ready to be learned (the latter example means that some prerequisite knowledge is not yet learned). The icon and the font of each link presented to the user are computed dynamically from the individual user model. They always inform the user about the type and the educational state of the node behind the link. Red means not ready to be learned, green means ready and recommended, and white means no new information. A checkmark is added for already visited sections.

The system knowledge about the course material comprises knowledge about what the prerequisite concepts are for any unit of the textbook. Often, when users have problems with understanding some explanation or example or solving a problem, the reason is that some prerequisite material is not understood well. In that case they can request prerequisite-based help (using a special button) and, as an answer to help request, the system generate a list of links to all sections which present some information about background concepts of the current section. This list is adaptively sorted according to the user's knowledge represented in the user model: more 'helpful' sections are listed first. Here 'helpful' means how informative the section is to learn about the background concepts. For example, the section which presents information about an unknown background concept is more informative then a section presenting information about a known concept. The section which presents information about two unknown background concepts is more informative then a section presenting information about one concept.

Authoring with interBook

The tool (provisional name is InterBook) is aimed to help the author to transfer a normal textbook existing in electronic form into an adaptive ET. To get the most benefits from it an author should start creating an electronic textbook with a hierarchically structured MS Word file. This section demonstrates a typical scenario of using this tool for the case when the original textbook is available as MS Word file.

Creating the list of domain concepts: Before starting to produce an adaptive ET, an author has to think about the list of domain concepts which will be used to annotate pages. An author does not have to have the list of all concepts before starting the work, it could be made when annotating the book.

Structuring and annotation: To let InterBook recognise the structure of a book, an author has to use the regular way of structuring an MS Word file. It means that the titles of the highest level sections should have a pre-defined text style 'Header 1', the titles of its subsections should have a pre-defined text style 'Header 2', and so forth. Then an MS Word file has to be annotated and indexed by the course author. An annotation is inserted into the file at the beginning of each section. The annotations have to be written using a special character style (hidden+shadowed). For each unit, the author can (but not have to) provide the set of outcome and background concepts.

Translation to HTML: The annotated MS Word file has to be saved in RTF formats and translated into an HTML file by the RTF2HTML program controlled by some specially designed settings. All annotations and section titles are translated into HTML comments which have a special format. The resulting 'InterBook file' is just an HTML file annotated with several kinds of special comments.

Parsing into LISP structure and Serving on WWW: When the InterBook server starts, it parses all InterBook files and builds the list of section frames. Each section frame contains the name and type of the unit, its spectrum, and its position in the original HTML file. The obtained LISP structure is used by InterBook to serve all the available textbook on WWW providing all advanced navigation and adaptation features. All content which the user will see on the screen is generated on-the-fly using the knowledge about the textbook, the user model, and HTML fragments extracted from the original HTML file. These features of InterBook are based on the functionality of he Common Lisp Hypermedia Server CL-HTTP.

Working with interBook

InterBook is expected to be used with Netscape 2.0 or 3.0 browsers. It uses advanced features of these browsers such as multiple windows and frames to provide the user with useful and powerful interface. Main windows used by InterBook are the textbook window and the glossary window.

The Glossary window is used to view the glossary: The upper part of the window is a list of glossary concepts. The lower part of this window is used to show the glossary entry for a concept. For each concept the system presents the concept description (if provided by the author), the list of section titles (selected from all available textbooks) which present the concept (i.e., which have it as an outcome concept) and the list of section titles which require this concept (i.e., which have it as a background concept). Section titles are clickable links which makes the corresponding section to be loaded to the Textbook window. The Textbook window is the most important window in InterBook interface. This window is designed to view the main content of a textbook, section by section. It is divided into frames performing different functions. Main frame of the Textbook window is the Text window. This window shows a particular section of the textbook which is called current section. For a terminal section the Text window shows the title of the section and the section itself. For a high-level section the Text window shows the title, the section preface (if existing) and the full table of content for the section (i.e. list of hierarchically structured titles of its subsections down to terminal level).

A vertical bar to the right of the Text window is the Concept bar. It is used to show the concepts related with the current section. All names of concepts on the Concept bar are links to the Glossary. The upper part of the Textbook window hosts the navigation center and the toolbox. The navigation center shows the position of the current section in the textbook: it lists the titles of all direct predecessors (father, grandfather, etc.) and all brothers of the current section. All names of the sections are clickable links. The navigation center serves for both orientation and navigation. The toolbox provides a set of buttons which are used to call additional windows (such as content window, search window, and prerequisite-based help window) which provides additional functionality.

The main idea behind tool is using concept-based indexing to make conventional educational material more intelligent and flexible. The idea of indexing is to provide the information about the content of each unit of conventional educational material by indexing this unit with related domain concepts. Previously, indexing was applied in three authoring contexts: CAI context, hypermedia authoring context and ITS authoring context. Indexing was originally suggested in CAI context who suggested a framework for indexing CAI frames by a set of topics which it covers. Such indexed sets of frames were not related to any pre-scribed order of presentation. They can be accumulated, stored in special libraries, and re-used by different authors to create their own courses. Later indexing was applied in hypermedia and ITS authoring area.

Artificial Intelligence in Education

The Artificial Intelligence (AI) in education developed intelligent tutoring systems (ITS). For the most part, ITS, like CAI systems before them, have attempted to implement traditional methods of learning and teaching. Drill-and-practice, and other variants in which students solve relatively short problems chosen by the teacher, have a proven pedigree in the classroom. Perhaps more important, ITS using a drill-and-practice method have generally aimed at well-defined and well-accepted goals for learning. These typically include factual knowledge and procedural skills, like algebra symbol manipulation, that are part of traditional school curricula, and that can be measured by existing standardized tests. Working with traditional methods of teaching and learning, and using traditional means of evaluating outcomes, the developers of ITS have tried to show that ITS can significantly improve the speed and quality of students learning. And, to some extent, they have been successful. However a looming paradox undermines these successes.

The technologies that make it possible to automate traditional methods of teaching and learning are also helping to create new methods, and to redefine valued educational goals. For example, new technologies can automate symbol-manipulation algebra and spelling correction, making these skills less important to learn, while increasing the importance of 'higher-order' skills required to do creative mathematics and writing. As a result, attempts to use new technologies in education to further traditional learning goals or traditional methods of teaching makes less and less sense. This situation poses tremendous difficulties to the development of effective educational technology applications.

Traditional goals and methods for learning are at least well understood and relatively well-defined. But new methods—for example learning through inquiry, collaboration, or visualization—and new goals for learning have not yet been agreed upon by the educational community at large, let alone fully operationalised. Crafting effective technologies for fixed learning goals and methods of teaching and learning is challenging enough. But is even more demanding when the target you are aiming at is moving. Microworlds and interactive learning environments (ILEs) are one response to these changes in the educational landscape. Generally, they are trying to implement an inquiry-based method of teaching and learning, perhaps helping to bring this method into the classroom on a large scale for the first time. However, at the same time, ILEs are involved in a shift of educational goals as well as methods. Its not simply a matter of providing tools for new methods of learning skills now taught in many classrooms.

In some cases, new educational goals focus on topics that are not part of traditional curricula, such as boolean networks and chaos, graph theory, and inquiry skills themselves. In other cases the focus is on traditional topics, like fractions or polygons, but the intent is to foster a deeper conceptual understanding of ideas that are usually taught as simple procedures. The movement from ITS to ILEs, and to mixed-initiative systems that represent a combination of both approaches, illustrates a general pattern in educational technology today. Virtually all important computer-based applications to education are not simply trying to teach traditional skills more quickly, efficiently or less expensively. Rather, like ILEs, they are participating in an attempt to change methods of learning and teaching and to redefine valued educational goals and learning outcomes. As a result, there is no reason to believe that the most effective uses of AI (or advanced technology in general) in education will happen quickly or without careful policy and planning.

In the short-term, technologies resembling many ITS—that aim at well-defined learning goals and that can be moved into classrooms with a minimum of disruption—will provide the most statistically significant improvements in student outcomes. Policies that support research based on their ability to generate such results in 'horse race' evaluations risk encouraging technology applications that miss longer-term benefits. On the other hand, policies which simply give researchers free reign to develop software that focuses on new methods of teaching and new learning outcomes also run considerable risks. The problems in developing these systems and moving them into education on a broad scale are not simply technical ones. The experience provides a case in point. When developing ITS for mathematics education, 75 per cent was spent on technical and research issues, but implementation required most of our time when we integrated ILEs into schools. As technology continues to transform the goals for student learning and to enlarge the range of methods for teaching and learning, implementation will require proportionally more effort.

In general, implementation tasks must develop new curricula, assessment methods and instruments, teaching practices and professional standards, and teacher education. These tasks cannot all be effectively done by any single group of researchers. Rather, believe that scaling up new technologies like ILEs will require a division of labour—different groups or projects working in a coordinated fashion to put together the technology, curricula, assessment tools, professional standards, and teacher training pieces of a package of broad educational reform. However, very little evidence of such coordination. Research in these areas is typically funded by disjoint government programs that provide few incentives or mechanisms necessary to engender needed cooperation. In the future it will be important to consider new policies that improve the communication between these groups.

A variety of policy options are worth examining, including larger consortium-based projects that include expertise in software development as well as teacher training and other key stakeholder groups, smaller separate projects that work together synergistically using new networking technologies, and incentives that bring high-tech companies into better cooperation with educational technology research and classroom practice.

Computer technologies are changing the practice of research and business, and—very slowly—the content and practice of education are beginning to follow suit. This chapter discusses how work in artificial intelligence (AI) is contributing new approaches to education and learning. The hallmark of AI applications in education is that they attempt to explicitly represent some of the reasoning skills and knowledge of expert practitioners, and to exploit that expertise for teaching and learning. In business growing evidence that information technologies are leading to substantial improvements in productivity by automating routine activities. Similarly, it seems that if we can impart basic cognitive skills of teachers to computers we might delegate some teaching to machines and thus improve educational outcomes. However, this will chronicle several ways in which such a theory vastly oversimplifies practice.

The main goal of this chapter is to review past and present trends in the applications of AI in education, the successes and failures of those applications to possible future applications. The chapter is a personal perspective in several senses. It selectively highlights a few important issues but makes no attempt to survey all key ideas in educational technology. Discussion is limited to two main applications of AI in education: intelligent tutoring systems and microworlds. Even more narrowly, compare these two approaches primarily in terms of their methods of learning and teaching—the procedures, principles, and techniques they embody to facilitate learning—and their learning outcomes or goals for learning—the particular kinds of knowledge and learning they help students acquire, or try to help them acquire.

A personal perspective because it illustrates many of its main points with reference to our own research at RAND over the past several years. Other research to support general points, but many outstanding systems and studies are mentioned only in passing or not at all. The organization is roughly chronological. The first section discusses the application of AI ideas in developing early intelligent tutoring systems, reviewing both their successes and limitations. These limitations motivate the relatively recent development of interactive learning environments and microworlds. The general reflections on the current state-of-the-art, and with some speculations on possible future directions for AI in education.

Intelligent tutoring systems

The development of intelligent tutoring systems for education over the last decade. We begin by reviewing the fundamental ideas behind these systems and illustrating them with reference to tutors we have developed. While knowledgeable readers will find this review familiar, it sets the stage for the following discussion of successes and failures.

The first (and still foremost) application of AI to education has been to build intelligent tutoring systems (ITS). ITS attempt to capture a method of teaching and learning exemplified by a one-on-one human tutoring interaction. For researchers in AI this method of teaching was a natural one to target first for several reasons. Drill-and-practice versions of one-on-one tutoring are relatively well-understood ways of communicating knowledge. This method of learning and teaching is widely accepted both by the educational community and by our culture as a whole. And it has achieved broad popularity for good reason. One-on-one tutoring allows learning to be highly individualized, and consistently yields better outcomes than other methods of teaching. Although many methods have been examined, no other has reliably yielded "2 sigma" improvements— usually over a full letter-grade—in student outcomes. Failure to attribute strong outcome improvements to other methods of teaching and learning may be partly a function of inadequate techniques for evaluating novel learning outcomes, as we elaborate below. However, regardless of evaluation problems, it is clear that one-on-one tutoring remains a 'gold standard' of learning. Although ITS differ in a variety of ways, most have a characteristic structure.

In most CAI systems and ITS students learn by working a series of relatively brief questions. In both cases the system plays the exclusive role of the task expert, controlling the selection of tasks or problems, while the student responsible for answering them. The system also plays the role of the critic, and in most ITS the system rather than the student decides when critical feedback will be supplied. The main differences between ITS and earlier CAI systems do not reflect differences in methods of teaching and underpinning philosophies of learning. Rather, they reflect engineering and psychological enhancements that permit ITS to tutor in a knowledge-based fashion. ITS represent some of the knowledge and reasoning of good one-on-one human tutors, and consequently can coach in a much more detailed way than CAI systems.

The heart of an ITS is its expert system. The expert system embeds sufficient knowledge of a particular topic area to provide 'ideal' answers to questions, correct not only in the final result but in each of the smaller intermediate reasoning steps. The expert system thus allows the ITS to demonstrate or model a correct way of solving the problem. Often, like a human tutors, it can generate many different answer paths or goal structures. The same detailed data structures that expert systems generate in modeling expert reasoning also permit ITS to explain their reasoning at arbitrarily detailed levels. For example, if a student needs an explanation of why or how an algebra ITS did a step in solving an equation, the system might first say that it used the distributive rule.

ITS coach as well as model expert problem-solving. In particular, they can monitor the student as he or she solves a problem and can determine if every step is right. Thus, while questions were the atomic unit of discourse in CAI systems, in ITS the basic unit is the individual reasoning step. To support this detailed coaching, ITS often create and update a student model. The student model reflects the correct rules the ITS thinks the student knows—ones that are also found in the expert system or in the ideal student model. But, since most students are not ideal, the student model often contains rules that are 'buggy'—invalid rules the ITS thinks the student believes. The ITS watches each step in the student's reasoning as he or she solves a problem. Each time the student makes an error, the ITS will diagnose the problem—possibly updating the student model—then attempt to remediate it with very detailed advice about how the expert system would do the step. This process repeats at every step in the evolution of a complete solution to a problem.

One part of most ITS that receives relatively little mention is the pedagogical component. While the expert system contains rules and knowledge that drive an ITS subject-specific performance, the pedagogical component is supposed to contain similar rules that encode expertise about tutoring itself—for example when to interrupt students and what kinds of information to provide them.

The algebra ITS have developed over the past several years illustrates many of the key features of intelligent tutoring systems. The ITS helps students learn freshman level algebra, focusing on equation solving and symbol manipulation. In different versions of the tutor the student can solve problems using symbols, operations, or commands. In the 'Symbols' version, students input new equations that lead toward a solution. Students can input equations either by typing or by using electronic pencil. In 'Operations' the student issues requests like add 30 to both sides of the equation. The different versions allow the student to focus on different levels in the rather complex hierarchy of reasoning skills that characterize even simple algebra. Students practice one level of decision-making, and the ITS takes care of other levels that the student is not concentrating on at a given time. For example, if the student says 'collect' the ITS will figure out what 'collect' means in terms of operations, then also do the appropriate symbol manipulation.

When the student creates steps in a solution he or she can develop multiple different solution paths that appear as different branches in a solution tree. Solution trees 'reify' the student's reasoning process by showing connections between steps. Such reification allows the student to easily compare different solution approaches, or to contrast a 'buggy' approach with a correct one. In this case, for example, the student's first (leftmost) attempt began by distributing and the second attempt uses the more elegant approach, by first collecting. This approach was suggested by the computer after a request for help from the student (the command that began this branch is in inverse video in the commands window to the right, indicating this step was done by the machine). The student can request explanations at increasing levels of detail. Like other ITS, the algebra tutor's main strength is that it permits coaching at an arbitrarily fine grain size.

The experimented with two very different pedagogical components in algebra tutor. The pedagogical policy permits high students control. The student decides when to ask for help, when to request the expert to do and explain, when questions should be tougher and easier. Another version of the system is at the other end of the pedagogical spectrum. It is completely tutor controlled; the tutor, not the student, decides what questions to give, and when to help the student.

Most ITS are still being used on a very small scale, and only a few have been tested widely. Of these, just a handful claim to improve students' outcomes in the classroom using standardised tests. Successful ITS have been mainly restricted to areas of mathematics and science, where it is both easier to build ITS and easier to measure learning outcome improvements. The algebra ITS has been tested on several occasions using introductory algebra classes at a local high school. In each fielding, one or more classes used the ITS and comparison classes learning the same curriculum, did not. Our evaluations have primarily focussed on the role of the tutor in improving traditional algebra learning outcomes. Specifically, we were interested in measuring improvements in solving symbolic equations, and on seeing whether students could benefit by reasoning separately about goals, operations, and symbols. Our best results indicate that students using the algebra tutor scored almost a letter-grade higher than comparison students for a more detailed discussion of curriculum and results.

In addition to enhancing students' outcomes in traditional algebra symbol manipulation, several evaluations of our algebra tutor have attempted to see if the tutor could improve skills not measured by most standardized tests. For example, might students using the algebra ITS improve their ability to model realistic situations with equations, as well as skills for manipulating and solving equations? Could they improve other 'higher-order' skills, like planning, debugging (fixing errorful solutions) and goal setting? However, these benefits come at a cost. To improve these skills we had to extensively restructure the standard algebra curricula in which ITS was embedded. For these pilot tests, crafting the software took less time than developing the non-computer materials and providing teacher training. These results an important general pattern. By adopting one-on-one tutoring, ITS have aspired to implement a very familiar, well-understood, and accepted method of teaching and learning.

At the same time, most ITS have aimed at equally familiar learning goals or outcomes. These typically comprise procedural skills, like algebra symbol manipulation, that are part of traditional school curricula. Such outcomes are relatively easily measured by the standardised tests that are used in most school curricula. Consequently, it is relatively straightforward to determine the success or failure of ITS in objective and broadly accepted ways. On the other hand, to the extent that ITS—or any technology—attempts to target more novel learning outcomes, it becomes both more difficult to measure success, and more demanding to implement the technology in traditional classroom settings.

Reasons for ITS successes

There has been surprisingly little reflection in the literature on the reasons why ITS have succeeded, and on why their successes have been limited. This kind causal analysis is important for several reasons. First As analysis of Anderson's Geometry tutor underscores, the actual reasons for success may not the ones initially expected. The ability of an ITS, for example, to finely tune instruction may be less important than the fact that it permits teachers to spend more time with slower students or that it increases student motivation. Second, a given ITS, or any other demonstration system, has limited value if not tied to some general observations or principles. The real importance of any tutoring system is a function of the principles of learning which it illuminates. Any system, viewed as a software product, is likely to have a brief life-span and will directly impact few learners.

However, principles of learning, validated through demonstration systems, add to the enduring knowledge of learning and teaching that can guide the construction of new generations of systems. They become part of an incrementally growing base of scientific and design knowledge. The only important principles on which ITS can impact are those that underpin cognitive theories of learning. For one thing, teaching principles and general interface design ideas are equally important, and may not be reduceable in any systematic way to learning principles. But we agree that a key contribution of ITS lie in the general truths they uncover or exemplify. From this perspective, then, several features or principles are responsible for the (admittedly limited) success that ITS now enjoy.

Probably the greatest strength of ITS are their ability to generate highly detailed feedback about problem solving—to micro-tutor. They can coach and model problem solving down to atomic levels of reasoning. Micro-tutoring is the main teaching principle ITS embody that distinguish them from earlier generations of CAI. The converse learning principle argues that learners need rich, variable granularity feedback. When learners accomplish a task they use their skills along with external tools to generate reasoning and visible performance. Although learning can happen with nominal feedback, generally richer feedback yields more accurate diagnosis of errors, thus faster learning.

The need for rich feedback is especially important when tasks are authentic and skills are embedded. Because so many skills may be used in the process of generating an answer or step, it may be difficult for students to locate their errors among many acceptable actions and to draw a general inference from the errors.

Tutor Control of Learning

Although some ITS, such the student-controlled version

of our algebra tutor, permit limited student choice, for the most part interactions with ITS are tightly controlled by the software. In most cases, the ITS selects the next task or problem, decides when the student needs support and feedback in problem solving, and determines the nature of the information the students receive. Students may tailor information; for example they may request more detailed explanations. But their latitude is usually highly circumscribed. The principle of high tutor control reflects an implicit belief that a competent tutor is usually in a better position to make decisions about what experiences and information students need to learn effectively than the students themselves. Of course, this assumes, at a minimum, that the tutor knows the content the students want to learn, and also knows the students' specific knowledge state—what they know, and what knowledge they lack—at any given time. The expert systems and student models of ITS attempt to provide this expertise and to thus meet the demands of high tutor control of learning.

In the tutor-controlled version of algebra tutor, for instance, feedback and help is triggered by an algebraic error. By organizing learning around small short-answer tasks, and by choosing tasks that are demanding for students, ITS attempt to maximize opportunities for impasses. But, like many ITS, tutor's decision-making in response to impasses is quite 'thin'. Interventions are immediate reactions to errors alone. For example, they are not conditioned by a plan to set up the learning experience beforehand or to help students define goals or plans. However, whether ITS reason extensively or not, virtually all reasoning attempts to recognise student impasses and overcome them. The learning principle that corresponds to teaching principle of impasse-driven coaching is to provide immediate feedback. Most ITS, implicitly or explicitly, are built on the premise that a good learning system will provide detailed feedback as soon as an impasse is detected.

ITS appear to contribute to effective learning outcomes, they substantiate the principles of micro-tutoring, high tutor control, impasse-driven coaching and providing rich and immediate feedback. However, although ITS are successful in part because they are consistent with various theoretical principles of learning and teaching, practical reasons may be equally important, if not more so. The simple fact is that ITS actually fit quite well into existing classrooms, easily filling the shoes of earlier CAI programs and integrated learning systems that have enjoyed at least modest success. ITS are congruent with existing classroom practice in at least two senses.

— They generally aim at learning goals or outcomes that are already embedded in traditional curricula—algebra symbol manipulation, programming, and geometry, for example.

— They adopt a popular method of teaching and learning. Most classrooms still combine lecture with drill-and-practice.

As a consequence, teachers have little trouble finding an effective role for ITS like our algebra tutor. They can usually be plugged into existing curricula with minimal change to course plans; for example, they often simply replace pencil-and-paper homework or drill-and-practice seatwork. It is important to note that not all software fits into classrooms so easily. As we elaborate below, many recently developed computer environments are more aligned than ITS with emerging standards for mathematics curricula which advocate new methods of teaching and learning and emphasize new goals for student learning.

While ITS have been somewhat successful on a small scale, several problems must be overcome before they have widespread impact. Various authors have discussed a wide range of limitations. Many of these challenges can be predictably factored by ITS component—limitations associated with the expert system, student model, pedagogical component, and interface. In this section we touch relatively briefly on just a few shortcomings that we believe are most fundamental and which may not be overcome simply through incremental improvements to various ITS components. In the next section we discuss how researchers applying AI to education are responding to these challenges.

Educational technologies can aim at a wide variety of learning goals or outcomes, from helping students learn skills in traditional subjects and curricula, to making new topics accessible to younger students, to facilitating deep conceptual understanding, to fostering metacognitive skills like debugging. Most ITS have focused on subjects taught in typical primary—and high-school level courses. In this context, probably the most significant limitation of ITS is that, to date, they can be developed only for a few topic areas. Effective ITS require virtual omniscience—a relatively complete mastery of the subject area they are to tutor, including an understanding of likely student misconceptions. Thus, the most successful ITS have been developed for simple closed worlds and procedural skills like solving short problems in mathematics, science, and logic. These are the easiest topics for which to build complete expert systems simply because cognitive science provides elaborate task analyses of competence in these areas.

Conversely, ITS have not yet been successful developed for less well-understood or well-defined subjects. These include a wide range of topics in history and social sciences, where natural language understanding would appear to be prerequisite for any effective ITS. But they also include areas in science and mathematics, such as those emphasized by NCTM. For example, cognitive science cannot yet provide a complete task analysis of expertise in posing novel problems, designing good experiments, or creatively applying the scientific method. Similarly, while ITS can help students practice the symbolic manipulation of equations, they cannot tutor the effective application of these representations in modeling real-world situations. As a result, it is current impossible to develop an omniscient expert system for these topic areas, let alone modeling student misconceptions. And, without an effective expert system, an ITS loses its educational leverage.

Subject competence limitations of ITS can be interpreted weakly or strongly. A weak interpretation agrees that effective ITS are currently limited to topic areas which are relatively simple, and perhaps of minor importance in emerging curricula. But a weak interpretation also argues that eventually ITS will be built for many of these more interesting topics, perhaps relying on new breakthroughs in the representation of knowledge provided by artificial intelligence and cognitive science research. On this interpretation, the subject limitations of ITS are little more than a reflection of the youth of the field. On the other hand, a strong interpretation of the competence limits of ITS argues that it may never be possible to develop ITS for interesting topic areas. One of the reasons that rote calculation and algebraic symbol manipulation are no longer highly valued parts of math curricula, for example, is that these computations can be automated. Since they can be done by machine, so the argument goes, they lose value as curriculum topics, while new skills (that perhaps presuppose these simpler ones) become increasingly important. In math, for example, schools are slowly reducing the time spent learning multiplication tables, while reluctantly increasing exposure to higher-order skills involved in finding and understanding abstract mathematical patterns.

The strong interpretation of the competence limits of ITS thus does not deny that new research in artificial intelligence will bring more topic areas in range for ITS. Rather it suggests that the very act of automating new kinds of reasoning will devalue them as curriculum topics. On this argument, the developers of ITS are caught in a 'catch 22' they can never escape. As ITS improve, the learning outcomes they can engender will expand accordingly; but the value of these outcomes will decline at the same time.

A second important limitation of ITS pertains to their restricted knowledge of teaching. Most ITS have very impoverished pedagogical components. Such components often comprise a collection of rules that just seem to work reasonably well in practice. There is no scientific encyclopedia of good tutoring heuristics to consult, let alone a principled theory of one-on-one tutoring from which specific heuristics might follow.

Cognitive science has not yet progressed to the point where it can offer good task analyses of pedagogical expertise the way it has articulated the reasoning in 'closed worlds' like symbol manipulation algebra, arithmetic, and chess. In short, the pedagogical component of ITS is an 'expert system' that cannot yet build.

Just as learning outcome and subject limitations have weak and strong interpretations, pedagogical limitations can also be viewed narrowly or broadly. The narrow interpretation, implied above, improve the pedagogical capabilities of an ITS need to enhance the rule-base that tells it when and how to coach students. On this interpretation, the basic structure of tutorial interaction—a method of teaching that emphasises one-on-one tutoring, and the more detailed principles of micro-tutoring and impasse-driven coaching— remains intact. All that is needed is to enrich the pedagogical knowledge base. In short, a weak interpretation suggests that we simply need to do a better job of implementing the method of teaching and learning that ITS are already pursuing.

A strong interpretation of ITS pedagogical limitations argues the problem is not merely that the prevailing one-on-one tutoring method is incompletely developed. Rather, this interpretation suggests a more fundamental problem—that ITS are constrained to a single method of teaching and learning while truly expert tutors can adopt different methods. However good ITS are at micro-tutoring, they are still limited to a drill-and-practice style of interaction. More generally, they lack the ability to tutor flexibly; to adopt different teaching methods when appropriate, and to permit students to use different learning styles. By contrast, competent one-on-one human tutors may shift methods depending on the needs of students and on other contextual factors. A session may begin in an apprenticeship mode, then shift into drill-and-practice, and finally into less constrained, student-centered inquiry. This meta level reasoning about appropriate teaching and learning methods is well beyond today's ITS.

The drill-and-practice method of teaching embedded in ITS appears to be more suitable for tuning existing knowledge than for conceptual learning of substantial pieces of new knowledge. This limitation, in part, reflects limitations in the cognitive science that underpins ITS. Psychological theory has accumulated a good understanding of how to remediate small 'bugs' in knowledge.

In the last several years, applications of AI in education have diversified; approaches are more fractured, and the field is certainly not as unified as five years ago when ITS dominated AI research in education. These new trends exemplify different responses to the difficulties encountered in developing and testing the first generation of ITS. Very broadly, while some recent research attempts to improve the one-on-one tutoring method of teaching associated with ITS, other work is investigating different methods of teaching and learning. This research is rethinking important principles of learning and teaching that should underpin education in general and the design of educational technology in particular. At the same time, new work is attempting to expand the range of learning goals and outcomes associated with AI-based systems for education. In some cases this means developing educational software for a more diverse set of subjects, but in other cases the targeted knowledge has less to do with the subjects learned than with the quality or depth of learning.

A substantial amount of work continues within the ITS framework. Different groups are attempting to improve the various components of ITS, to develop applications in increasingly complex subjects, and to make ITS more cost-effective to develop by providing 'shells' and other system-building tools that institutionalize the basic structure of ITS. In doing so, this research largely holds fixed the drill-and-practice method of teaching, while attempting to enhance learning outcomes or goals either by improving the quality of tutoring of subjects already within range of ITS, or by expanding the range of subjects ITS can tutor.

While many early ITS focused mainly on simple topics in high school mathematics, recently ITS have been developed for more advanced topics in mathematics and science. ITS have also grown beyond mathematics and other more formal subjects to include topics in history, language and social science. Similarly, ITS have diversified beyond public school curricula to topics in training and vocational education.

Intelligent Tutoring Systems

There were multiple efforts to use World-Wide Web WWW facilities for distance learning. At the same time most existing educational WWW applications use the simplest solutions and are generally weaker and more restricted than existing 'on-site' educational systems and tools. A number of powerful technologies which prove to be very effective for 'on-site' education are still not implemented within the WWW framework. One of these technologies is Intelligent Tutoring Systems (ITS) technology. ITS use the knowledge about the domain, the student, and teaching strategies to support flexible individualised learning and tutoring.

ITS technologies to hypermedia and WWW

The most obvious way to bring ITS to WWW is to port some existing ITS technologies to WWW. The most relevant technique for that is intelligent knowledge sequencing and problem sequencing. Intelligent knowledge sequencing implies adaptive selection of the next topic to be learned using the student model and the knowledge about the learning material. Intelligent problem sequencing in the narrow sense implies choosing or generating the next problem for the student to solve, which should be most relevant to his level of knowledge and skills. In a broader sense it implies adaptive sequencing of all kinds of teaching operations—examples, tests, problems, questions, etc. In a hypermedia systems intelligent knowledge sequencing is usually considered as intelligent sequencing of hypermedia pages or hypernodes.

In addition to regular (prescribed) hypermedia buttons or active fields the student is provided with dynamic 'intelligent button' called 'next' or 'teach-me' which activates knowledge sequencing mechanism. This button brings the student to the hypernode, which is most relevant to him from system's point of view. Intelligent problem sequencing is usually implemented by the same way—the student is provided with a dynamic button which activates sequencing mechanism. As a result the student is presented with the most relevant problem to solve for the currently studied topic or for the course in general. Implementation of intelligent sequencing within hypermedia framework brings new quality by combining student-directed and guided learning. It provides some solution for 'getting lost' problem of hypermedia: the learner who can hardly find his own way in hyperspace can now use system guided navigation. At the same time it provides some benefits over traditional 'directed' ITS style of teaching: the students who are not satisfied with system-directed sequencing can use hypermedia style of browsing the learning material.

Integration of ITS and WWW hypermedia technologies provides a new quality in one more sense: it opens the way to some new intelligent techniques, which are based on both ITS and hypermedia paradigms and which are new in the ITS domain. Adaptive hypermedia is a good example of such a technique. As in general hypermedia system, the educational process here is driven by the student. The difference is that adaptive hypermedia systems can use the student model and some other knowledge typical to ITS to adapt its work to the given student. In particular, it can be used to guide the student implicitly. Adaptive hypermedia systems bridge the gap between computer-driven tutoring systems and student-driven educational environments. They combines free browsing with personalization and can support not just two ends (as classic ITS and hypermedia), but all the continuum of learning modes between pure system-controlled and student-controlled. What can be adapted in adaptive hypermedia are the content of a hypermedia page and the links from a page to related pages. We distinguish these two techniques of adaptation and call the first technique adaptive presentation (or content-level adaptation) and the second technique adaptive navigation support (or link-level adaptation). Adaptive presentation is the most popular and the most studied way of hypermedia adaptation. With adaptive presentation the content of a hypermedia page is generated or assembled from pieces according to the user's class and knowledge state.

Generally, qualified users receive more detailed and deep information, while novices receive more additional explanation. Two popular application areas for adaptive presentation are adaptive hypermedia-based help in knowledge-based systems and on-line documentation systems. By adaptive navigation support we mean all the ways to play with visible links which can support hyperspace navigation. In current systems, three kinds of adaptive navigation support have been suggested and implemented: hiding a part of links, adaptive ordering of visible links, and adaptive annotation of visible links. Hiding of a part of visible links was used in. Ordering of visible links according to some user-valuable criteria (the more close to the top, the more relevant the link is) can give user a hint when selecting the next link to follow. This technique was suggested in, and the positive experimental results.

A promising and flexible technology for adaptive navigation support is adaptive annotation of visible links (augmenting links with personal dynamic comments in any form). Adaptive annotation can use icons or other visual cues to reflect the state of the related nodes according to user knowledge and goals.

Bibliography

Anderson, A H, Newlands, A, Mullin, J, Heming, A. M., Doherty-Sneddon, G and Van der Velden, J., 1996, "Impact of Video-mediated Communication on Simulated Service Encounters", *Interacting With Computers*, 8, 2, pp.193-206.

Bauer, J. W., and Rezabek, L. L., 1993, *Effects of Two-way Visual Contact on Verbal Interaction during Face-to-Face and Teleconferenced Instruction*, In *Art, Science, and Visual Literacy: Selected Readings from the Annual Conference of the International Visual Literacy Association*, 24th, Pittsburgh, PA, September 30-October 4, 1992.

Burow-Flake, E., Kocher, D., Reiser, A., 2000, *Changing Students, Changing Classroom Landscapes: Meeting the Challenge in the Small Liberal Arts Institution*, in L. Lloyd (ed.), *Teaching with Technology, Rethinking Tradition*, Medford, NJ: Information Today, Inc.

Cohen, J. A., Castner, M. H., 2000, *Technology and Classroom Design: A Faculty Perspective*, in L. Lloyd (ed.), *Teaching with Technology, Rethinking Tradition*, Medford, NJ: Information Today, Inc.

Duhaney, D., 2000, Technology and the Educational Process: Transforming Classroom Activities, *International Journal of Instructional Media*, 27(1), pp.67-72.

Duffy, T., Jonassen, D., (eds.), 1992, *Constructivism and the Technology of Instruction: A Conversation*, Hillsdale, N., Lawrence Erlbaum Associates.

Gilbert, S. W., 1997, *Teaching, Learning, and Technology*, Change, 217, 4 6. Guernsey, L., and Young, J. R. 1998, June 5.

Kirby, E., 1999, "Building Interaction in Online and Distance Education Courses", *Paper presented at the Society for Information Technology and Teacher Education International Conference*, 10th, San Antonio, TX, February, 1999.

Phye, G., 2000, "Engaging Technology and Learning Opportunities: Technology Assessment Tools", *Paper presented at the Annual Meeting of the American Educational Research Association*, New Orleans.

Roberts, L., 1996, *A Transformation of Learning: Use of the NII for Education and Lifelong Learning*, In D. P. Ely & B. B. Minor (eds.), *Educational Media and Technology Yearbook 1995/1996*, pp. 50-66, Englewood, CO: Libraries Unlimited.

Index